What grows here?

grows here?

Volume 2 **Problems**

what
favorite plants for better yards
grows
here?

Volume 2
Problems
Jim Hole

H
HOLE'S

Printed in Canada   5   4   3   2   1

National Library of Canada Cataloguing in Publication

Hole, Jim, 1956-

      What grows here? : favorite plants for better yards / Jim Hole.

Includes index.

Contents: v. 1. Locations - v. 2. Problems.

ISBN 1-894728-02-5 (v. 1).-ISBN 1-894728-03-3 (v. 2)

      1. Gardening. 2. Plants, Ornamental. I. Title.

SB407.H64 2004   635.9   C2004-901319-X

Printed by McCallum Printing Group Inc.

Image on page 32 used courtesy of Advance Orchards

Hole's
101 Bellerose Drive
St. Albert, Alberta, Canada
T8N 8N8

Lone Pine Publishing
10145-81 Avenue
Edmonton, Alberta, Canada
T6E 1W9

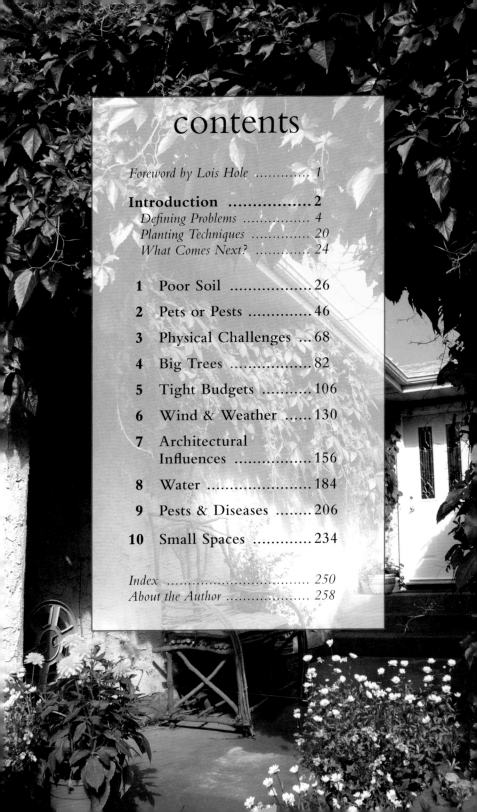

contents

DEDICATION

This book is dedicated to my mother, Lois Hole—

THE BEST TEACHER I EVER HAD. 1929 – 2005

FOREWORD

I don't remember the exact moment when people first started coming to me with their gardening problems, but it was probably during the days when we ran a pick-your-own vegetable garden. As people came to buy their cucumbers and peas, they'd often bring along questions: "How come your tomatoes aren't black on the bottom like mine?" "Why don't my squash ever grow as large as yours?" "Why isn't my cucumber producing?"

When we started the greenhouse operation, the questions came with more and more frequency. Pretty soon I was writing a column for the local newspaper and travelling across the province (and eventually the continent) giving gardening talks. I even had segments on CBC television and radio for a while, and more often than not, the topic focussed on one problem or another—and as time went on, the questions grew more complex. So complex that, inevitably, some of them started to reach beyond my area of expertise. Since my focus was always on promoting the best varieties rather than solving pest and disease problems, I finally told one caller, "Listen, here's what you do: call my son Jim at the greenhouse, and he'll tell you exactly what the problem is and how to solve it." And I gave out Jim's number over the air. It seemed like a good plan to me; after all, he'd been dealing with all kinds of problems in the greenhouse for years.

Well, the phone started ringing off the hook at Jim's desk, and he was a little taken aback by it all. Jim's duties at the time involved plant production on the growing range rather than dealing with large volumes of customers. But when I got back to the greenhouse that day, I could see that he'd really enjoyed discussing such a wide range of problems with all kinds of gardeners because he was learning as much as his callers. Since I was taking on new, non-gardening challenges and Jim found the exchange with gardeners challenging, he gradually took over the radio and television duties, as well as my gardening columns and books. Jim's been having fun with people's plant problems for a while now, and he's loving it—just as I knew he would.

–LOIS E. HOLE
NOVEMBER 2004

Introduction

Over the years, I've been asked to answer a lot of questions about gardening. Once people know that you have a greenhouse business, sooner or later, even in casual conversation, a plant question will emerge. I really enjoy the exchange of information that occurs when people ask questions during my radio or speaking appearances and at our greenhouse, but far too often for my liking the questions are prefaced with remarks such as "I've got a brown thumb," or "I kill every plant that I try to grow." Statements like this tell me how prevalent gardening problems are and just how frustrated many gardeners become.

We all want success in whatever endeavour we undertake, but it seems that we see problems in the garden as major obstacles—I hear time and again from gardeners who are embarrassed to admit that some of their plants have died. We need to change this outlook by reminding ourselves that no matter how much experience you may have, gardening is a continual process of discovery. Give yourself a break if something doesn't work out as planned.

Plant problems are no different from any other problem; they cause stress, frustration, and even damage to your bank balance. But the process of addressing these problems brings great rewards: a better-looking yard, appreciation of nature, closer ties to your particular plot of land or simply a healthy dose of exercise. Yes, problems are aggravating, but they also present opportunities.

This is the second book in the *What Grows Here?* series. The series purpose is twofold: to provide choices of plants to meet your garden's needs and to capture the valuable ideas exchanged between gardeners and professionals. In *Volume 1*, we focused on specific locations in the yard. *Volume 2* is about dealing with the problems associated with creating and maintaining a satisfying landscape and growing beautiful plants.

If there's one thing I've learned during my years on the farm and in the greenhouse, it's that there's a solution for almost every gardening problem. It might not be the one you expected, but you just may discover a brand new approach—and ideally, one that will fit your needs perfectly.

Defining problems

For the purposes of this book, we define a problem as any condition in the yard that is unpleasant, inefficient, unproductive, unsafe or unattractive. In the most basic sense, a problem is anything that makes the gardener (or perhaps his or her neighbours) unhappy.

Problems can range from the refreshingly simple to the frustratingly complex; they can be merely annoying or potentially devastating. But no matter the precise nature and scale of the problem, success in this context has only one definition: in the end, the gardener must be satisfied with the solution.

Attitude is Everything

Attitudes in gardening tend to parallel attitudes in other aspects of our lives. When you encounter a problem, you can simply ignore it and hope it goes away or tackle it head on with the hope of solving it quickly. Or you can take the hybrid approach, as most of us do, ignoring some problems and attacking others, depending on our level of tolerance.

I know some gardeners who are fearless experimenters. They have a "rip and replace" attitude; if something doesn't work, rip it out and try a different plant. Others see a dying or poorly performing plant as a failure, and such failures often have an emotional effect—not to mention a financial one. I've known gardeners to spend $20 to save a $5 plant, simply because the trauma of seeing the plant die is far worse than the financial cost of keeping it alive.

Problems demand solutions, but isn't it better to avoid a problem in the first place? That's where I hope this book will help: by choosing the right plants for the right situation, you can prevent many problems before they occur.

The owner of this tree has created a problem by failing to remove the entire collar used to stake the tree when it was first planted.

Problems of Our Own Making

Even with the best attitude towards problems, we're all fallible, and sometimes we make situations more difficult than they have to be. A lot of our woes can be attributed to poor planning; we buy a tree that will eventually grow too large for the yard, or we plant an invasive perennial that's fated to take over the garden. Or we procrastinate, letting the plants go an extra day without water, checking for diseases or insect pests just a little later than we should have…and the garden deteriorates under our noses. We react by overcompensating, spending loads of cash on new plants or pesticides in a blind panic, hoping that something, *anything,* will fix the problem.

Good old common sense is the best antidote to these self-inflicted miseries. Before taking any action, stop and think about what you're doing—consider the long-term implications, whether planting, amending the soil, removing plants or applying pest controls. And when a problem does crop up, make sure you actually understand its nature before devising a solution.

Types of problems

Sometimes the nature of a problem is obvious, as when a tree grows too large for the yard. Sometimes the cause can be more difficult to pin down, as when the foliage on your roses starts to turn brown. Problems often have multiple causes, and breaking problems down into digestible chunks helps make analysis easier. In this book we've grouped the most common- types of problems into ten chapters.

Soil

Soil plays a huge role in determining whether or not your plants will flourish, and soil-related conditions are very often the cause of many problems with plants. Virtually all plants grow in soil; it's their lifeblood. And yet, all too frequently soil quality is an afterthought, when it should be a gardener's top priority. Know your soil—is it heavily clay based or on the sandy, loose side? Chapter 1, *Poor Soil,* beginning on page 26, will help you understand the importance of the composition and pH of the soil in your yard. It will also help you determine which plants will grow best there, and what to do if you can't grow what you want with the soil you have.

All too frequently soil quality is an afterthought, when it should be a gardener's top priority.

Soil ph

Over the years, I've seen many problems that seemed intractable, yet the solutions were very simple. Frequently, the problem arises from one simple misunderstanding of how a particular plant grows. I can remember one fellow who was extremely proud of his beautiful, thick green lawn. He was meticulous with his watering, fertilizing and mowing, yet one spring his lawn began to change from emerald green to dull, ominous yellow. He assumed that it was underfed and simply applied more fertilizer. Within days his lawn responded, not by recovering, but by growing even worse.

When I discussed the problem with him, it didn't take long to discover its cause. He'd used 16-20-0 fertilizer on his lawn for many years, and this particular fertilizer is very acidic. Kentucky bluegrass (the most common lawn grass, and the one he was growing) hates acidic soil. The 16-20-0 worked for years only because his soil was quite alkaline to begin with, but eventually the repeated dosages dropped the soil pH into the acidic range, enough to harm the grass. Once this point was reached, each new application of fertilizer only compounded the damage. Adding a bit of lime and switching fertilizers solved the problem, returning the lawn to its former glory.

Dealing with pets means compromising, perhaps even giving up prized growing space to accommodate a dog run.

Animals

Animals are nice to have around, but a deer isn't quite as welcome when it's snacking on your prized shrubs or a dog quite so amusing when it's trampling favourite perennials. Dealing with animals often involves compromise. My mother used to sow seed twice as thick as required, knowing that various animals were bound to take their share. Putting up barriers, planting unpalatable varieties, applying odiferous deterrents—there are ways to strike the right balance between your gardening desires and the presence of pets and wildlife. Chapter 2, *Pets or Pests* (beginning on page 46), deals with these concerns from an animal and garden lover's point of view.

Trees protect our homes and yards from wind and the hot sun—but they present gardening challenges (above).

The design of the garden at the Calgary branch of the CNIB accomodates the abilities of the partially sighted (right).

Physical Challenges

It is not very often that you see the issue of physical limitations mentioned in gardening books. Chapter 3, *Physical Challenges* (page 68) reminds us that many of us have problems that can make traditional gardening difficult. We need to recognize that some plants and some garden styles are more demanding than others—the key is to work within our abilities and adjust our gardening practices accordingly. For example, if you can't reach over your head to water or deadhead flowers, try having a helper mount hanging baskets on a pulley system for you. If you're not limber enough to remain on your hands and knees weeding for hours at a time, then use planters or raised beds. Don't let physical challenges prevent you from enjoying your garden.

Big Trees

I love big trees, but they come with their own set of issues. There's always a price to pay for that huge maple—extra shade, fewer nutrients and mois- ture for other plants, extra pruning…not to mention the tendency of big trees to grow where they want, even if that means their branches start in- terfering with overhead power lines. If you want big trees in your yard, you've got to learn how to balance *their* needs with *your* needs. Check out chapter 4, *Big Trees*, on page 82 for more inspiration.

Budget Woes

Some folks believe that you have to spend a lot of money to have a beautiful landscape. I disagree. I have seen many stunning yards that were developed on a shoestring budget. What the gardeners who create these noteworthy landscapes have in common is a willingness to share knowledge and resources, and an ability to apply good design principles. They're patient and they use the money available to them wisely. You don't have to break the bank to get great gardening results. In Chapter 5, *Tight Budgets*, we share some excellent tips for getting the most out of your gardening dollars.

PREVENTION
The Best Medicine

In the garden, an ounce of prevention is worth a hundred pounds of cure; so don't wait for problems to get out of hand. Scout the garden regularly, watching for pest and disease problems. Look toward the future when you plant, anticipating plant growth rates and your own changing needs. Are you planning to have children, or are they on the verge of moving out? Thinking about getting a pet? Building a deck when you can afford it? Making the right choices now can solve a heck of a lot of work in the future.

Weather

Daily and seasonal variations in weather can have a huge impact on your plants. Plants must deal with temperature fluctuations, lengthy cold periods, fierce winds, driving rain and pounding hail. If you are a risk taker, testing the limits of a plant's endurance to local climate conditions is one of the most interesting and rewarding challenges a gardener can accept. If you hate to lose plants to weather-related causes, then stay within the comfort zone of tried-and-true plants for your area—but be aware that nature's going to throw you a curve ball now and then.

If you live in Zone 2 and want to grow peaches, you have a problem: the winter is too cold for the trees to survive. If you live in Zone 11 and want to grow tulips, you have a different problem: the winter isn't cold enough for the bulbs to undergo vernalization. If a plant can't survive or grow to its full potential in your climate, you need to make different planting choices (you often have many more options than you think) or modify the way you grow out-of-zone plants (such as using a greenhouse or protective mulch). Chapter 6, *Wind & Weather,* starting on page 206, will provide you with lots of tips on growing within your zone.

Shaping the (Almost) Perfect Yard

When my wife and I first considered purchasing what is now our home, people thought we were nuts. The entire yard was dominated by big, straggly trees, dying grass and ugly, deteriorating fences. The house—itself a little odd-looking, like a big sugar cube—appeared lost in the bush. We knew it was going to take a lot of work to turn this strange place into an attractive landscape, but even through the obscuring brush, the potential was undeniable.

So, with a mixture of careful planning and spur-of-the-moment inspiration, we attacked each problem. Unhealthy trees were chopped down, fences were repaired, camouflaged with plants or replaced with hedges, dead grass was replaced with new turf, flowerbeds were created and planted up, and large pots full of bedding plants, vegetables and flowering bulbs were added to the deck, the sidewalks and even the roof. Today, we think our yard looks pretty darn good, even if the architecture is still a little off the wall. (And frankly, I like it that way.)

Naturally, different gardeners would have solved our problems in different ways; after all, everyone's home should be a reflection of their own personal style. We can offer recommendations for all sorts of problems, but in the end, you'll have to make the final choices.

Aggravating Architecture

There are aspects of our yards and the surrounding landscape that we can't change: the placement of a garage, the presence of unattractive overhead utility lines or the unappealing design of the next-door neighbour's garden. In these situations the demands on your creativity can be intense, but sometimes immutable objects aren't quite as bad as you think. Chapter 7, *Architectural Influences*, reminds us that by choosing the right plants, we can make even the most troublesome spots a lot more attractive.

Moisture

Chapter 8, *Water* (page 184), discusses the water-related problems we run into when we miscalculate how much of it each plant needs, fail to consider how to get it to them or forget to water at all. Applying the right amount of water, and doing so consistently, is one of the best things you can do to keep your plants growing well and your landscape looking beautiful. Choosing plants based upon their individual need for moisture is a positive step towards environmentally sensitive gardening.

Diseases and Insect Pests

Of all the problems gardeners face, diseases and insect pests are the ones I hear about most often. But if you understand even a little about their life cycle and habits, you'll be far better equipped to handle them than gardeners who just instinctively reach for chemical sprays or rip out plants. Knowledge is power and that ability to make appropriate, effective choices trans-lates to saved money, effort and time. In Chapter 9, *Pests & Diseases* (page 206) we've grouped together questions that are frequently aimed at our staff. Our intent is to sim-plify the origin, treatment and prevention of the most prevelant disease and insect problems.

Fireblight is a disease that must be dealt with quickly to prevent its spread.

If you pay attention to your plants, problems are less likely to get out of control.

Space

All yards are finite; there's room for just so many plants to live together comfortably. If determining which plants will take the best advantage of limited space is a challenge that you face, turn to Chapter 10, *Small Spaces*, beginning on page 234. When dealing with space issues you'll find that it takes some trial and error to find the right plants, based on the growing conditions in your area. Avoid the common mistake of choosing plants that you know will grow too large for your allotted space. It's unrealistic to believe that you can keep them pruned to a manageable size, unless you are truly prepared to prune often, and are aware of how that plant will look in twenty years if kept pruned to half of its mature height.

The perfect solution

Some problems are more serious than others. Once you've evaluated the difficulty, then you have a choice of approaches. There are times when there is only a single viable solution to a given problem; sometimes, you're faced with a number of possibilities.

A solution can be as simple as choosing the right plant for the right location, and then spending the necessary time and effort properly maintaining that plant. A tough, robust plant has a far better chance of fighting off pests, diseases and unexpected frosts than one suffering from a lack of water or nutrients. Healthy plants have a smaller chance of pest or disease attack, and therefore less need for chemical sprays as a solution. Be consistent with your watering and feeding routines, and pay attention to the specific needs of your plants, some will need to be pinched or pruned periodically, while others will need extra micronutrients for optimum growth. When matching a plant to a location, consider the plant's water and nutrient needs, its full-grown size, rate of growth, disease resistance and bloom/fruiting period. And perhaps most importantly, choose a plant that will thrive in that location while meeting your aesthetic goals.

Some problems involve more than just choosing the right plant, and require landscape or structural solutions before plants can even be considered. These solutions can be costly, as in the case of retaining walls, but they may be absolutely necessary. When things are really bad, you may need to take drastic measures. Sometimes that means ripping out your plants and starting over, or removing and replacing your soil. If an apple tree is infested with fireblight, you're better off to get rid of the tree and start over with a fireblight-resistant cultivar than to battle the infection endlessly. The surgical approach can be a bit labour intensive and costly in the short term, but it can save you a lot of headaches in the long run.

Viky and Ed Gartner take full advantage of the few sunny spots in their shady backyard.

Slow and Steady

Some solutions take years to evolve; a privacy screen of clematis or cedars may take several seasons to become fully effective, for example. Alternatively, you may need to use bedding plants to cover up a bare spot while working on a long-term landscaping project. How patient are you? A row of 30-centimetre-tall cedars will grow into a huge, vigorous hedge...*eventually*. Some gardeners have no problem waiting a few years for the garden of their dreams. You'll simply have to decide whether you're a member of that group.

The Process of Problem Solving

Solving any problem involves a process. I take two basic steps before I even consider applying a solution.

1 Identify the Problem or Problems

Be sure that you've correctly identified the problem. If the spots on your tomatoes are caused by bacteria, spraying the plant with a fungicide is a waste of time and money. Similarly, spraying for mites won't do much to diminish the aphid population.

2 Assess Your Resources

Decide how much the problem bothers you, and how much time, money and effort you're willing to devote to the problem. If you can live with the fact that the growing season in your area isn't long enough for your kiwis to fruit, but you still enjoy the flowers and foliage, then don't spend a whole bunch of time trying to extend the season. On the other hand, if your crab apple tree is dropping fruit all over your lawn and you can't stand the cleanup anymore, it might be time to remove the tree, despite the labour involved. Now you have to decide whether to take on that work yourself or to hire a professional.

Tools & Tips

No gardener is an island, and solving problems is much easier when you use all the resources available. I have a pretty extensive library of books, periodicals and personal notes that I've used to solve many tough problems. When that doesn't work, I check the Internet, visiting college and university websites in particular; their biology and horticulture departments often have valuable research that gardeners can put to use in their own yards.

Of course, there's nothing like the voice of experience when it comes to solving a problem, which is why I'll often consult one of the experts here at the garden centre. I'm lucky enough to work just down the hall from some very experienced horticulturists, with decades of combined experience covering almost every gardening subject under the sun. While most gardeners don't have that kind of instant access, most greenhouse workers and operators are happy to share their knowledge with the public—it's good for business, and we all want to see our communities filled with great-looking yards.

Substitutions

This book offers plant choices as solutions to specific problems. In most cases we've recommended specific plants because we've used them to solve problems of our own. Of course, other varieties of the same plant may work too; don't be afraid to experiment. Use our choices as a guide and if one of our selections isn't available in your area, ask your local garden centre staff about other varieties. And again, don't be shy about using all the resources available today—the Internet, gardening books and magazines, horticultural societies and your experienced friends and neighbours.

Debra and Herb Zechel's garden is a lush, shady oasis comprised of winding paths through beds of their favourite plants.

planting techniques

We can create problems for plants right at the outset by not planting them properly. The following planting techniques are designed to nip planting-related problems in the bud.

1 Loosen and amend the soil.

If a plant has the right growth medium, it's already got a good defence against potential problems. Oxygen is as critical for plant growth as water, but we tend to forget this point. Adding organic matter enriches the soil and increases pore space, so that air can penetrate more easily. Compaction is one of the biggest problems when it comes to healthy root growth, and adding organic matter helps alleviate this problem, too. And don't forget—it's a lot easier to amend the soil before you plant than trying to fix it after your plants are in place!

2 Dig a hole for the plant according to its type.

For perennials, the planting hole should be twice as wide and as deep as the pot the plant comes in. For trees, shrubs and roses, the hole should be the same height and three times as wide as the rootball. Roots will grow only where the balance of water, oxygen and nutrients is correct. Spending extra time preparing the planting hole leads to healthy root growth and, in turn, reduces plant problems.

3 Remove the plant from its pot.

Handling varies, depending on the type of container.

Plastic Pots: Always remove plastic pots before planting. (This may sound rather obvious, but we have on occasion talked with people who have made the mistake of not removing a plastic pot, perhaps thinking the pot will decompose.) Slash the sides and bottom of a tree or shrub's rootball. Roots that may have circled around the inside of the pot will rebranch from the cuts and grow outward.

Fibre Pots: Conventional wisdom says that fibre pots should not be removed. That is certainly true in the case of spring-pottted plants—plants that have had their roots trimmed in the field and then are potted up for early sale. Disturbing their rootball by removing the fibre pot when planting can have detrimental results, so we advise our custom-

Shane Neufeld, Hole's nursery manager, advises customers to always take the time to dig and prepare the correct size of hole according to the plant's type.

Roughing up or slashing a compacted, tight rootball will force rebranching in an outward direction.

Do not remove burlap completely from trees. Open it and set it along the sides of the hole.

ers to cut off the pot's rim and slash its sides and, if it appears that the rootball will fall apart, to stop and back fill. The pot will gradually decompose.

I suggest removing a fibre pot completely only if the the tree or shrub you're dealing with has been actually grown in its fibre pot (called container-grown plants by the industry). Why leave any obstacles to root growth in place, even if the fiber will eventually decompose? Better to give the roots a head start by getting the pot out of the way—provided the rootball is

intact enough to handle the pot's removal.

Not sure whether the plant you're purchasing is spring-potted or container grown? Just be cautious and as you slash the pot's sides carefully observe how far the root system has advanced. Its size should be your guide as to whether or not you should remove the pot.

Balled and burlapped trees: Generally we don't remove the burlap completely. The reasons are twofold: we don't want to disturb the rootball by having the soil fall away, and sometimes trees and shrubs are simply too heavy to make lifting and removing the wrap practical without snagging roots. Instead, position the plant in the hole, open the burlap and lay it in the bottom of the hole. You can then cut away as much of it as possible—provided you don't disturb the rootball. The remaining burlap will gradually decompose.

Jim's View

Proper preparation of the planting site and high-quality soil are far more important to healthy plant growth than 20-20-20 or any other fertilizer. Although fertilizers can aid in plant growth, use them sparingly, and only after you've taken all the proper planting steps first.

4 **Plant to the right depth.**

Put the plant in the hole. The rootball should sit just below ground level. If necessary, refill the bottom of the hole with soil to ensure that the plant is planted to the level it was in its pot. Never plant a tree or shrub deeper than its potted depth, as this can lead to poor rooting. (An exception to this rule is grafted tender roses: the graft needs to be 8–10 cm below the soil line. If active green growth is visible at the graft, leave a depression in the soil until fall.)

Fill the hole with remaining soil, but don't pack the soil around the roots; just pat it down gently to eliminate any large air pockets. Small spaces are essential so that air can reach the roots. Leave a slight depression around the plant. Stake any tree over 1.5 m tall for one year.

5 **Add fertilizer and water well.**

Feed the new plants a solution of 20-20-20 fertilizer. Newly planted trees and shrubs need about 5 L of solution for every 30 cm of height or spread. If you're using mycorrhizal fungi, water the planting area with 20-20-20 at half its normal rate.

Light in This Book

Plants require differing amounts of light, and sometimes the issues surrounding light intensity can be confusing. For example, morning sunlight can be just as intense as afternoon sun, but plants that love shade will do better with morning rather than afternoon sun. What gives?

The biggest problem with afternoon sun is that it is accompanied by more heat than morning sun. The temperature on a sunny morning may be around 20°C, but in the afternoon, it could climb to 30 plus. If a plant is slightly water stressed, the stomata (pores the plant uses to "breathe") close up. With no moisture escaping the leaves, the plant can't cool itself, and leaf temperatures increase drastically. So it's not so much the light intensity that damages foliage; it's the combination of intense light and intense afternoon heat that does the deed.

Here's a breakdown of what the light requirements we've used in this book mean.

Sun Plants in this category need full sun all day long for best performance. Fruiting plants, for example, need full sun to produce large yields.

Sun to p.m. sun Plants in this category will bloom and look fine if they receive afternoon sun, from noon until evening.

Shade Shade plants prefer shade all day.

Shade to a.m. sun These plants require cooler, less intense light. They can tolerate sun from morning until noon, but can't stand hot afternoon sunlight. They will also thrive in dappled light, as through a tree canopy.

Sun or shade These plants adapt equally well to sun or shade.

what comes next?

The next section of this book is divided into ten chapters that group the most common types of problems into categories. Here you will find plant listings that deal specifically with each kind of problem.

Each listing may include basic information about use, blooms, fragrance, soil requirements, preferred locations and light requirements. Plants are listed by common name, series and/or variety in the following categories: Annuals, Bulbs, Fruit, Herbs, Perennials, Roses, Vegetables, Trees & Shrubs and Water Plants. If you are looking for a specific problem or plant, use the index to help with your search.

We've selected a broad variety of the best plants for each problem. In some cases we have suggested a series and in others a single variety within a series. Plants have generally been recommended for use on their own, and some may be successfully combined with the other choices presented, at your discretion. We've successfully grown our recommended species in Zone 3A—for more on zones see pages 11 and 130.

Over the years, my attitude towards problems has mellowed. I remember how angry my brother Bill and I used to get when we lost a crop—especially if it was due to some dumb mistake we'd made. But lately, I've come to see problems as chances to flex my creative muscles. There's nothing quite as satisfying as solving a problem that has been plaguing me for years.

Of course, I still have my moments—no gardener ever seems to be completely satisfied. So the next time you're tempted to tear your hair out as you yell, "What the HECK grows here?" just take a deep breath, relax and read on.

1
Poor Soil

Dishing out the Dirt

Modify it or learn to live with what you have. The story with soil is simple.

When I was growing up on the farm, I was often frustrated dealing with the nuances of the various types of soil in our fields. One field was composed of clay loam; another was silty with lots of organic matter and a huge amount of peat. I knew that if I planted carrots in the peaty soil, the seedlings could easily break through the surface and the crop would be good, whereas if I planted those carrots into the clay loam, a crust could form after the spring rains and the seedlings would have great difficulty breaking through.

On the other hand, the carrots in the peaty soil tended to dry out much more quickly than those in the clay loam, so in the end there might not be any difference in yields between the two fields at all. It all depended upon when the rains came.

Because these fields were enormous, changing the soil quality was a daunting task. It takes tonnes of organic matter and many years to enrich that much clay soil; in these circumstances, adapting the crop to the soil, rather than the other way around, was the best plan for us.

The same holds true in yards. If you have a huge swath of poor soil and a limited budget, you may have to learn to live with those conditions and choose plants that match the soil. The good news is that many plants really will thrive in all types of soil. But if the area is large but still manageable, amend it with organic matter, and if you have a small spot with bad soil, then I say dig it out and replace it with high-quality loam.

Tailor the solution to the scope of the problem. This approach will make for a better garden and a happier gardener.

IN THE GARDEN

Bruce Keith and Leslie Vermeer's back-yard had poor soil. Two huge spruce trees dominated the small yard and the other plants struggled in deep shade for nutrients and moisture. The trees dropped several centimetres of needles every year, and the lawn between them was patchy at best. This situation was discouraging but one area showed promise: a two-tiered raised bed running along the side of the garage.

Getting rid of the trees wasn't an option, so Bruce decided to renovate the raised beds by removing all the plants and replacing half the soil with new rich loam amended with organic matter. He read books and visited garden centres to discover which plants had the best chance of thriving in the shady area and even managed to salvage some of the plants he had removed.

Renovating that one bed drastically improved the yard's look, giving it an attractive focal point. Bruce and Leslie learned that many of their garden's problems could be solved with good soil, some hard work and a little research.

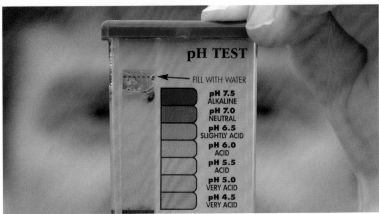

Knowledgeable garden centre staff can help interpret soil test results and suggest a course of action.

We have recently purchased our first home. In exploring the garden, we noticed a lot of the plants seem to be struggling. We spent a few dollars on a soil test kit and discovered that the soil is acidic. What grows here?

VIRTUALLY ALL SOILS CONTAIN TRACE AMOUNTS of elements such as aluminum, iron and zinc. When soil is more basic (or alkaline) than acidic, these elements pose no problem. But when the soil is too acidic, a greater percentage of these metals become soluble and are more likely to be absorbed by the plants in toxic amounts. As well, many beneficial soil micro-organisms, which convert elements like nitrogen into nutrients that plants can use, don't function well in very acidic soils. You can leave your soil as it is, choosing to grow only plants that prefer moderately acidic to neutral soils (such as those listed below) or you can add horticultural lime to increase the pH level. Fortunately, it's easier to raise pH than it is to lower it. A knowledgeable staff member at your local garden center will be able to help you determine the amount of lime to add based upon your soil test results. Apply dolomitic lime, as it contains both calcium and magnesium (two important plant nutrients), and be sure to buy a fine grade of lime that will react more quickly in the soil.

FRUIT

Blueberry 'Northland'
Vaccinum
This variety produces high yields (4–7kg) of tasty berries in late July/early August that are great to eat fresh or to cook with. Blueberry shrubs also provide striking foliage colour in the fall. Prefers moist, acidic soil and benefits from winter snowcover. Height: 1m; spread: 1.5–2m. Sun.

PERENNIALS

Columbine Meadow Rue
Thalictrum aquilegifolium

Wonderful background plant. Does best in cool, damp summers. Clustered, pale purple flowers appear in early summer on a clump-forming habit. Blue-green, columbine-like foliage. Prefers moist, organic, fertile and acidic soil. Height: 60–90cm; width: 45cm. Sun to P.M. sun.

White Beardtongue
Penstemon digitalis 'Husker Red'

An upright plant with dark burgundy-bronze foliage and cream-white flowers (sometimes tinted purple)—irresistible to hummingbirds. Blooms in summer and is drought tolerant, preferring fertile, well-drained soil. Height: 50–75cm; width: 20–30cm. Sun to P.M. sun.

TREES & SHRUBS

Birch 'Paper'
Betula papyrifera

A beautiful feature tree for large yards. Spectacular in winter with hoar frost coating small branches. A large, oval-headed tree with attractive bright white bark that often peels. Produces catkins in spring. Height: 15–20m; Width: 10–15m. Sun.

Hydrangea 'Annabelle'
Hydrangea arborescens

A very showy shrub—cut down to ground in early spring. Produces incredibly large, ball-like blooms from August to September. Moist soil is essential. Height: 60–90cm; width: 60–90cm. Sun to A.M. sun.

Rhododendron 'Roseum Elegans'
Rhododendron catawbiense

A spectacular spring-flowering shrub. A hardy variety, suitable for a sheltered site. Bright purple-pink flowers bloom in late spring. Requires moist, acidic soil. Height: 1.5–2m; width: 1.5–2 m. Sun to P.M. sun.

Rhododendron 'Roseum Elegans'

Columbine Meadow Rue

Birch 'Paper'

Pale leaves with prominent veins can be an indicator of iron deficiency caused by soil that is too alkaline.

I live in a prairie province and have a problem with many plants looking pale and "veiny." I understand from my neighbour, a gardener of long experience, that the soil is commonly alkaline in our area. What grows here?

"PALE AND VEINY" could easily describe a plant suffering from an iron deficiency. In alkaline soils, many essential nutrients (such as iron) remain bound up as insoluble compounds that plants have a hard time absorbing from the soil. When an iron deficiency occurs, it's usually because the soil isn't acidic enough to dissolve the iron present into a form that the plants can absorb. Some plants, such as those in the rose family (which includes roses, strawberries and raspberries) have high requirements for iron and don't like alkaline soil. In fact, most plants grow best in a slightly acidic soil (pH of 6.2–6.5). Before you rip out your plants or choose to amend the soil, do a soil test to confirm your suspicions. You will learn as much from this one step as you would from years of trial and error. The results will help you understand and deal with your soil chemistry. If your soil is alkaline, add garden sulphur to lower the pH or grow plants that thrive in moderately alkaline soils.

ANNUALS

Salpiglossis, Royale Series

An exotic-looking bedding plant. This series produces a colour mix of extra large, trumpet-shaped flowers. Great used in large containers or as a striking garden plant. Makes an excellent cutflower. Height: 60cm; spacing: 20–30cm. Sun to P.M. sun.

Strawflower 'King Mix'

Splendid, everlasting flowers with large, full flower heads in shades of rose, silvery-rose, yellow & silvery-white. The papery blooms make superb cutflowers displayed fresh or dried. Heat and drought tolerant. Height: 90cm; spacing: 20–30cm. Sun.

PERENNIALS

Creeping Baby's Breath
Gypsophila repens

A drought-tolerant, mat-forming plant with a creeping habit. Use in a rock garden or raised bed. White flowers appear in late spring to early summer. Prefers sharply drained, deep, alkaline soil—avoid winter wet. Height: 15–20cm; width: 30–50cm. Sun to P.M. sun.

Creeping Baby's Breath

Strawflower 'King Mix'

Salpiglossis, Royale Series

Pincushion Flower
Scabiosa caucasica

This long-stemmed, summer blooming plant produces blue, white or lavender pincushion-like blooms—attracts bees and butterflies. Great in a mixed border or wild garden, preferring fertile, well-drained soil. Clump-forming in habit. Height: 45–60cm; width: 45–60cm. Sun.

Rock Soapwort
Saponaria ocymoides

A reliable and popular plant for the rock garden, producing pink to soft purple flowers in late spring to early summer. Requires sharply drained, fertile, gritty soil and has a mat-forming, spreading habit. Height: 10–15cm; width: 30–45cm. Sun to P.M. sun.

White Checker Mallow
Sidalcea candida

A clump-forming perennial with an upright habit. Produces spikes of long lasting, white flowers in summer that make good cutflowers. Tolerates all soil conditions except wet sites, but prefers moist, well-drained, fertile, deep soil. Avoid winter wet. Height: 60–90cm; width: 45–60cm. Sun to P.M. sun.

TREES & SHRUBS

Amur Maple 'Ventura'
Acer tataricum ssp. *ginnala*

This variety of amur maple is less prone to chlorosis than others. Produces brilliant orange-red fall colour. Has a strong tendency to be single stemmed—can be trained to a bonsai-like form. A beautiful feature for small yards. Fragrant blooms in spring. Height: 4-6m; width: 5m. Sun.

Pincushion Flower

Amur Maple 'Ventura'

Rock Soapwort

White Checker Mallow

Cedar 'Brandon'
Thuja occidentalis

Medium to dark green, dense foliage on an upright form of cedar. Use as a feature, singly or grouped. Makes a striking screen. Best grown in a moist, humid site. Height: 9–10m; width: 2–3m. Sun to P.M. sun.

Russian Almond
Prunus tenella

This lovely feature shrub is useful in mass plantings, along foundations or in mixed shrub beds. Considered a very consistent bloomer, producing deep pink, almond-scented, rosette-shaped flowers in early spring, prior to leaves emerging. Height: 60cm–1.5m; width: 60cm–1.5m. Sun to P.M. sun.

Willow 'Laurel Leaf'
Salix pentandra

A fast-growing and extremely hardy tree for open areas. Does well in moist sites and prevents soil erosion on banks. Produces very dark green, glossy foliage on an attractive form. Height: 10–15m; width: 7–10m. Sun.

Willow 'Laurel Leaf'

Russian Almond

Cedar 'Brandon'

Sandy, quick-to-drain soil and dry conditions make the careful selection of plants essential to success.

We live in southern Alberta where we receive very little rainfall and snowfall is extremely inconsistent from year to year. The soil in my flowerbeds is quite sandy and pretty quick to drain. We regularly have watering bans imposed on us by the county. What grows here?

YOU MUST CONSIDER SEVERAL FACTORS when choosing plants for your location: the amount of rainfall, the inability of the sandy soil to retain water and unreliable snow coverage to protect plants over winter. You can take steps to amend the soil to increase water-holding capacity and add nutrients. You can also apply mulch to slow moisture loss, keep the soil cool and insulate plant roots during winters when there is little snow cover. As for selecting the best plants, take a good look around your community. You'll be amazed at how many native plants have wonderful ornamental value. Many varieties of these plants are sold in garden centres and will meet your site's needs admirably.

ANNUALS

Gazania 'Tiger Mix'

A heat-loving annual that thrives in dry borders and rock gardens. This blend is an alluring mix of uniquely striped daisy-like flowers, including creamy-white blooms with rose stripes, bright yellow flowers with red stripes and other striking combinations. Drought tolerant. Height: 20–25cm; spacing: 15–20cm. Sun.

Portulaca, Sundial Series

Portulaca thrive in hot, dry borders and rock gardens, providing consistent, reliable colour in very hot conditions. This series produces 4–5cm, rose-like flowers in shades of yellow, cream, orange and mango. Height: 15cm; spacing: 10–15cm. Sun.

Gazania 'Tiger Mix'

Portulaca, Sundial Series

PERENNIALS

Asiatic Lily
Lilium 'Cancun'

Asiatic lilies are unmatched for wonderful blooms in the summer perennial bed. These clump-forming plants are pest resistant and hardy, producing blooms that make excellent cutflowers. Cancun displays canary-yellow flowers with orange tips in summer and prefers fertile, well-drained, organic soil. Height: 90cm; width: 30–45cm. Sun to P.M. sun.

Cushion Spurge
Euphorbia polychroma

This spurge forms a neat mound and never spreads from its allotted space. Bright chartreuse-yellow bracts appear in spring. Tolerant of poor soil but prefers well-drained, sandy soil in a hot and dry location. Height: 40–60cm; width: 40–60cm. Sun.

Asiatic Lily 'Cancun'

Cushion Spurge

Moss Campion
Silene acaulis

Forms an attractive carefree evergreen, mossy mat, topped with pink flowers in late spring to summer. For best flowering, grow in poor, gritty, sharply drained soil. Also called cushion pink. Height: 2–5cm; Width: 20–40cm. Sun to P.M. sun.

Blue Lyme Grass
Elymus hispidus

A tuft-forming, cool-season grass with arching, blue-grey foliage—excellent feature or contrast plant. Produces seed heads in summer. Prefers moist, sharply drained, fertile, organic soil but is very tolerant of dry conditions and poor soil. Height: 70–120cm; width: 40–60cm. Sun to P.M. sun.

Purple Gas Plant
Dictamnus albus v. *purpureus*

One of the longest living perennials, *Dictamus* produces an abundance of fragrant pink flowers in late spring to early summer. The plants are late to come up in the spring; do not disturb too early. Thrives in dry, moderately fertile, well-drained soil. Clump-forming in habit. Height: 75–90cm; width: 60–75cm. Sun to P.M. sun.

TREES & SHRUBS

Broom 'Cyni'
Cystis nigricans

Stunning in bloom and great for hot and dry locations. Flowers for three weeks or more, displaying showy yellow blooms on a compact form. Prune in spring to encourage bloom clusters. Thrives in well-drained, sandy soils. Height: 1m; width: 1m. Sun.

Purple Gas Plant

Moss Campion

Blue Lyme Grass

Juniper 'Prince of Wales'
Juniperus horizontalis

A lovely spreading juniper for rock gardens, acting as a great groundcover that drapes over walls and around rocks. Fast-growing with trailing branches and bright green foliage that often turns a purplish hue in winter. Height: 10–15cm; width: 3–4m. Sun.

Russian Olive
Elaegnus angustifolia

A round-headed, small tree that is also sold in shrub form. Silvery leaves and dark bark contrast well with evergreen backgrounds. Very fragrant, tiny, yellow blooms appear in June. Thrives in a hot, dry site. Height: 6–10m; width: 6–10m. Sun.

Juniper 'Prince of Wales'

Russian Olive

Broom 'Cyni'

The investment you make in topsoil now will affect the success of your garden for years to come.

We have a new home with no landscaping in place. The builder provided about six centimetres of topsoil but beneath that layer is compacted clay. We're not sure we can really afford to bring in truckloads of soil. What grows here?

YOU NEED TO KNOW THAT SIX CENTIMETRES of topsoil is simply not enough. Most plant roots—even grass roots—go deeper. The compacted clay soil that lies beneath the thin layer of topsoil doesn't allow movement of air and water and is difficult for plants to root in. There is little point in going to the expense of purchasing plants, sod or grass seed if there isn't enough soil. Look at it this way: the investment you make in topsoil now (which may not be as much money as you think) will affect the success of your garden for many years to come. If you can't afford to bring in enough topsoil to cover the entire yard, bring in enough to fill just the planting beds to a depth of 30 centimetres depth and landscape only a section at a time. There are plants that are more than tolerant of thin, poor soils, such as those found in mountainous regions (they actually perform poorly if grown in rich, deep soil) but most gardeners don't desire an entire yard of alpine plants. The plants listed here will be somewhat tolerant of thin or clay-based soil, but even these will perform better in deeper soil.

ANNUALS

Poppy 'Shirley Double'
Excellent in mass displays. Double, delicate flowers in shades of pink, red, salmon and scarlet. Allow to self-seed. Height: 40–50cm; spacing: 20–30cm. Sun.

PERENNIALS

Himalayan Fleece Flower
Persicaria affinis 'Border Jewel'

A long-blooming evergreen ground-cover, producing spikes of pink flowers aging to burnt red from early summer to fall. Foliage turns red in fall. Grows in a moist or dry area but prefers moist, fertile soil to produce a denser mat of foliage. Height: 15–25cm; spacing: 60–90+cm. Sun to P.M. sun.

Sedum
Sedum 'Autumn Joy'

A lovely, undemanding plant with succulent foliage. Displays clustered, deep pink flowers fading to copper-red in late summer to fall. Prefers well-drained, moderately fertile soil. Clump forming in habit. Height: 45–60cm; width: 45–60cm. Sun to P.M. sun.

Hawthorn 'Snowbird'

Alder 'Mountain Alder'

TREES & SHRUBS

Alder 'Mountain Alder'
Alnus tenuifolia

Grown as either a single or small, multi-stemmed form, this tree has striking greenish-bronze bark and is lovely covered in frost on a winter's day. Great for wet sites. Height: 9–10m; width: 6–7m. Sun.

Hawthorn 'Snowbird'
Crataegus x *mordenensis*

A beautiful, round-headed feature tree, great for small yards, screens or near decks as it is fruitless and almost spineless. White, fragrant, double blooms appear in spring. Height: 6m; width: 4–5m. Sun to P.M. sun.

Spiraea 'Snowmound'
Spiraea nipponica

A great accent or feature shrub. Displays dark blue-green foliage on a dense form that is covered in white blooms in May. Prune after blooming when required. Height: 90–150cm; width: 90–150cm. Sun to P.M. sun.

Himalayan Fleece Flower 'Border Jewel'

Spiraea 'Snowmound'

Although peaty soils are low in nutrients and tend to hold water, there are plants that will thrive in these conditions.

I live near a marshy slough and even though my property is above the flood plain, the soil has a lot of peat moss in it. Prairie grasses and willow grow prolifically but I'd like to add some other plants. What grows here?

PEAT MOSS IS SOLD BY THE TRUCKLOAD at garden centres every spring, and no wonder—it can hold a vast amount of water relative to its weight. In fact, some types of peat moss—sphagnum, for example—can trap twenty times its weight in water. Not surprisingly, given their origin, peaty soils can become quite waterlogged, holding water at the expense of oxygen, often leading to poor rooting. Soils that are typically high in sphagnum peat moss, such as yours at the edge of a bog, are very low in nutrients and minerals. To improve drainage and tilth, and add nutrients, take the time to amend the beds you want to plant with good-quality topsoil. Plants in the *Aracacia* family tend to do quite well in soils that are peat rich and acidic, and some vegetables also grow well in peaty soil. (If you travel in northern Canada, you'll see vegetable gardens planted in ditches along roadways, where favourites such as potato, turnip and cabbage thrive in the peat.) You'll need to add lime to bring the pH into the right range for most other plants.

ANNUALS

Meadow Foam 'Fried Eggs'

This low, spreading annual displays delightful single flowers with egg-yolk yellow petals tipped in white. A moist location is best. Height: 15cm; spacing: 10–15cm. Sun to P.M. sun.

PERENNIALS

Bunchberry
Cornus canadensis

This evergreen groundcover is good for naturalizing a shady area. Cream flowers in summer are followed by bright red, edible berries in fall. Prefers moist, acidic soil. Height: 10–20cm; width: 30+cm. Shade to A.M. sun.

Umbrella Plant
Darmera peltata

This interesting plant thrives in moist, boggy soil but will tolerate dry periods. It has a slow, spreading habit and produces large, rounded, dark green leaves that turn red in fall. White to pink flowers appear in early spring. Height: 60–90cm; width: 60–90+cm. Sun to P.M. sun.

Yellow Flag Iris
Iris pseudacorus

Ideal for planting in wet areas. Clump-forming in habit and will aggressively spread to cover large areas. Yellow flowers appear in early summer. Prefers wet, fertile, organic soil. Height: 75cm–1.6m; width: 45–60cm. Sun to P.M. sun.

TREES & SHRUBS

Azalea 'Northern Hi Lights'
Rhododendron

This variety in the Northern Lights series produces creamy-white, fragrant blooms in spring before leaves appear. The flowerbuds are hardy to -40°C. Thrives in acidic, moist soil. Prune after blooming. Height: 90–100cm; width: 90–100cm. Sun.

Chokeberry 'Autumn Magic'
Aronia melonocarpa

A really lovely shrub with fragrant, clustered white blooms in spring followed by clusters of purple fruit. Produces striking red and orange fall colours. Height: 1.5–2m; width: 1.5–2m. Sun.

Bunchberry

Umbrella Plant

Chokeberry 'Autumn Magic'

A sloped yard with fast-draining soil may be challenging but it can yield stunning results.

Our front yard is on a slight slope and the soil is rocky, gravel-based and quite low in organic matter. We find that water drains away very quickly and rather than continue to water quite so frequently or to choose to completely redo the yard, we'd like to grow plants that will thrive in the existing conditions. What grows here?

ROCKY, GRAVEL–BASED SOIL drains so quickly and is so poor in quality that many favourite gardening plants can't access sufficient moisture or nutrients from it. One door closes…another opens. Sure, gravelly soils don't hold a lot of moisture, but the plants that do grow in such soil tend to be less prone to root diseases, and they're much tougher plants in general. While we tend to think that compost, well-rotted manure and rich topsoil are nature's gifts to gardening, and that most plants are a homogeneous bunch of chlorophyll junkies, many are quite content to sip from their environment rather than guzzle. Alpine species in particular are "lean machines," preferring the conditions your front yard offers. You certainly can work with what you've got, but you could also consider amending small pockets of the landscape on a smaller scale to grow any favourite plants that require a richer, more moisture-retentive soil. Choose plants in a wide range of forms and heights, and use combinations of bulbs, annuals, perennials and even the odd tree and shrub.

Fall Bulbs

Striped Squill
Puschkinia scilloides libanotica 'Alba'

Clusters of bell-shaped, pale blue flowers with a darker greenish-blue strip appear in early spring. Plant in clumps or drifts of 25–50 bulbs—excellent in rock gardens, woodland gardens and informal borders. Can be planted to naturalize in lawns. Height: 15–20cm; plant 8cm deep, 4–5cm apart. Shade to A.M. sun.

Perennials

Creeping Baby's Breath
Gypsophila repens

A drought-tolerant, mat-forming plant with a creeping habit. Use in a rock garden or raised bed. White flowers appear in late-spring to early summer. Prefers sharply drained, deep, alkaline soil—avoid winter wet. Height: 15–20cm; width: 30–50cm. Sun to P.M. sun.

Lupine
Lupinus

Clump-forming plants with stiff stems supporting spiked, summer-blooming flowers, available in vibrant colours. Prefers well-drained, moderately fertile, sandy, slightly acidic soil. Leave to self-seed. Height: 75–150cm; width: 30–40cm. Sun to P.M. sun.

Creeping Baby's Breath

Striped Squill

Lupine

Clematis
Clematis hirsutissma

A great little rock or alpine garden clematis—tuft-forming in habit. Purple flowers in late spring to early summer. Prefers moist, well-drained, fertile soil. Height: 70cm–1.2m; width: 45–60cm. Sun to P.M. sun.

Perennial Dusty Miller
Artemisia stelleriana 'Boughton Silver'

Artemesias are excellent choices for poor soils. This variety is perfect for edging, in rock gardens or as a fast-growing groundcover. A very dense, woolly evergreen with silky-soft, silver-green, lobed foliage. Do not trim back

in fall. Prefers well-drained, alkaline, poor, dry soil. Height: 15–30cm; width: 60–75+cm. Sun to P.M. sun.

Spring Adonis
Adonis vernalis

Very attractive yellow flowers resembling buttercups bloom atop mounding, fern-like foliage in early spring. Dislikes being disturbed. Prefers fertile, well-drained, alkaline soil. Height: 15–30cm; width: 20–30cm. Sun to P.M. sun.

Perennial Dusty Miller

Spring Adonis

Old Fashioned Bearded Iris

TREES & SHRUBS

Caragana 'Weeping'
Caragana arborescens 'Pendula'

A great heat-tolerant feature plant for use in shrub beds or rockeries. Produces masses of yellow blooms in early summer on graceful weeping branches. Quite tolerant of poor, fast-draining soil. Height: graft dependant; width: 2–3m. Sun.

Juniper 'Cologreen'
Juniperus scopulorum

This variety of juniper is upright in habit and narrow and cone-like in form, making it useful for framing entrances or as a feature plant. A nice addition to rock gardens and small yards, requiring little or no shearing to maintain its shape. Height: 5–6m; width: 1.5–2m. Sun.

Spiraea 'Anthony Waterer'
Spiraea japonica

A heat-tolerant shrub with unusual bluish foliage that contrasts well with blooms. Dark pink flowers appear in midsummer for three to five weeks. Height: 90–100cm; width: 90–100cm. Sun to P.M. sun.

Tamarisk 'Pink Cascade'
Tamarix ramosissima

This shrub, commonly used as a background plant, thrives in poor soil. Pretty green, feathery foliage displays masses of pink blooms in summer. Height: 1–3m; width: 1.5–2m. Sun.

Tamarisk 'Pink Cascade'

Spiraea 'Anthony Waterer'

Caragana 'Weeping'

2
Pets or Pests
The Animal World

Learning how to live in harmony with large and small animals can be a measure of our maturity as gardeners. Part of the reason we garden is to foster a closer relationship with nature, including our pets—and perhaps the occasional pest. Whether it's the family dog, a wandering deer or a hungry rabbit, animals pose a special challenge to gardeners. How do you make your desire for a beautiful garden a reality while dealing with the often destructive habits of animals?

Reasonable animal control is as much a part of gardening as planting, weeding and harvesting. The fruit and ornamental trees on our family farm have faced regular devastation from porcupines, rabbits, skunks, deer, beavers, gophers, moles and mice—and seeing your plants ruined by foraging animals can be pretty tough on the blood pressure. Fortunately there are humane ways of dealing with such pests. We've trapped porcupines and released them into the wild, used plastic trunk protectors to save the bark from beavers and mice, installed netting around particularly delectable plants, and used tall fences to keep larger animals at bay.

We've found that accommodating pets requires an individual approach. My brother Bill and sister-in-law Valerie have had a number of dogs over the years, each with its own quirks. Their German shepherd loves peas, so Valerie simply plants extra. Their chocolate lab enjoys digging and lying in the soil beneath trees, and she frequently tracks dirt into the house. Bill and Valerie's response was to lay down a thick layer of mulch over the bare soil. The dog still lies in the shade but she doesn't dig anymore. In both cases, a compromise was reached to suit the needs of both the animals and their owners, and the garden looks great.

Flora and fauna go hand in hand. If you truly want to foster that closer relationship with nature, you may have to reach some compromises of your own.

IN THE GARDEN

Pat Lewis and Matt O'Reilly share their garden with Meaghan, an active golden retriever.

Meaghan's relentless patrols around the yard's perimeter resulted in worn-out grass and Pat's prized delphiniums being crushed.

Pat devised a plan that could accommodate both her desire for a beautiful yard and the dog's need to meet and greet passers-by. Matt installed sidewalk blocks along the inside edge of the fence line to create a path on three sides of the yard, and then backed flowerbeds along that path. They framed them in with landscape ties, raising them about 30 centimetres off the ground. Pat then installed tall perennials and shrubs, planted so thickly that the dog path isn't even visible. Her plants now flourish undisturbed and Meaghan is free to roam.

A happy pet and a very attractive, functional garden compensated for any loss of planting space. Pat and Matt's innovative solution shows the benefits of a little imaginative and inclusive thinking.

Unattractive dog runs can be softened and disguised by growing vines on the enclosure and tall plants in front of it.

We have a chain-link dog run situated along the sunny side of our house. We want to disguise it and provide shade for our dog without attracting too many bees. What grows here?

I N ADDITION TO CONSIDERING SHADE for your dog and avoiding stinging insects, you must also deal with the fact that the high salts and ammonia in dog urine burn plants. The best solution is to plant a border or bed half a metre away from the outside edge of the dog run. This way you are not dealing with the effects of dogs urine and there will be some distance between your dog and any plant that may attract bees. If you choose large enough shrubs or install a free-standing trellis on which to grow vines, the issue of shade can also be resolved. Some people grow perennial vines up their chain-link fences, but avoid the overly floriferous types if bees are a concern.

ANNUALS

Amaranthus 'Love Lies Bleeding'

Amaranthus caudatus

A superb feature plant that is quite
striking in backgrounds. Long, dark
red and trailing rope-like flowers make
interesting cut or dried flowers. Height:
90–150cm; spacing: 35–45cm. Sun.

PERENNIALS

Feather Reed Grass

Calamagrostis x *acutiflora*
'Karl Foerster'

One of the best clump-forming grasses
to grow as a feature plant that adds
height in a mixed border. Light pink
seed heads fade to tan in late summer.
Leave stems in place for winter interest. Prefers moist, organic soil. Height:
90–150cm; width: 30–45cm. Sun to
P.M. sun.

Big Petal Clematis

Clematis macropetala 'Rosy
O'Grady'

Produces a lush, pest-free screen; very
hardy. Grow as a climber with support,
a groundcover or trailing over walls.
Bell-shaped, pink-mauve flowers appear in spring, followed by attractive
seed heads. Do not cut back. Prefers
well-drained, fertile soil and cool roots.
Height: 3–5m; width 1–2m. Sun.

Ground Clematis

Clematis recta 'Purpurea'

This clump-forming clematis is na-
tive to central and southern Europe. It
has bronze-purple foliage and fragrant
white flowers in midsummer to fall.
Grow at the back of a mixed border.
Prefers fertile, well-drained, moist soil.
Height: 90–100cm; width: 60–90cm.
Sun to P.M. sun.

Feather Reed Grass

Big Petal Clematis 'Rosy O'Grady'

Amaranthus 'Love Lies Bleeding'

Virginia Creeper
Parthenocissus quinquefolia

This versatile vine will easily cover a fence, wall or tree stump. Provide support for this vigorous climber. Ivy-like foliage turns brilliant red in fall. Green-white flowers appear in summer, followed by ornamental blue-back fruit. Do not cut back in fall. Prefers fertile, well-drained soil. Height: 5–10m; width: 2–3+m. Sun or shade.

TREES & SHRUBS

Barberry 'Rose Glow'
Berberis thunbergii var. *atropurpurea*

Extremely tolerant of heat and especially striking planted en masse or used as a contrast shrub. Yellow blooms appear in May and June and are followed by red fruit. Unique rose-pink mottled leaves mature to deep purple and in fall turn pink-purple. Height: 90–100cm; width: 60–90cm. Sun.

Caragana 'Russian Globe'
Caragana frutex 'Globosa'

A nice, tight rounded form, perfect for rock gardens and small shrub beds. Medium to light green foliage on a slow-growing and extremely hardy plant. Heat tolerant and tolerant of high soil salts. Height: 60–90cm; width: 60–90cm. Sun.

Dogwood 'Silver & Gold'
Cornus stolonifera

A very nice contrast plant that combines well with other shrubs to make an attractive mixed screen. Beautiful

Dogwood 'Silver & Gold'

variegated form with bright yellow bark that is attractive in winter. Height: 2–3 m; width: 2–3m. Sun to P.M. sun.

Juniper 'Wichita Blue'
Juniperus scopulorum
Great for large shrubs beds, rock gardens or used as screening. This fast-growing, cone-shaped juniper displays brilliant silvery-blue foliage. Can be made more compact with annual

shearing. Height: 5–6m; width: 1.5–2m. Sun.

Salt Bush
Halimodendron halodendron
This hardy and adaptable plant produces greyish-green foliage and dark pink blooms in early summer. Very tolerant of dry, poor, saline soils. Height: 2m; width: 1–2m. Sun.

Juniper 'Wichita Blue'

Salt Bush

Barberry 'Rose Glow'

Having your toddler eating out of your bed of pansies isn't the best idea, but the delicate flower petals are quite edible.

We are facing two challenges this year in our garden. Our toddler is tasting his way through the world and so is our new puppy. We don't want to grow anything that might be poisonous if consumed by either! What grows here?

THE DOSE MAKES THE POISON. This is an axiom of Paracelcus, the father of toxicology. What it means is that everything, taken in large enough quantities, will eventually poison you. Believe it or not, even too much pure water has resulted in deaths, a condition known as hyponatremia. The point is that there has to be sufficient poison entering one's body to cause injury. Practically speaking, some of the most notoriously poisonous plants, such as foxglove, lily-of-the-valley, ornamental rhubarb and monkshood, taste so awful that children and pets spit them out as soon as they get a tiny taste. Heck, you can't even get kids to eat their broccoli, much less a potentially poisonous datura! Having said that, there is no substitute for the vigilance of a focused parent or a conscientious pet owner. Here we've listed just a few of the many plants that are considered non-toxic.

ANNUALS

Marigold, Gem Series

Tagetes marigolds make good accent plants. The pretty blooms are edible and may be used in salads. The Gem series produces masses of small, single flowers and lemon-scented, lacy foliage on compact plants. Height: 30cm; spacing: 15–20cm. Sun.

Snapdragon, La Bella Series

Snapdragons are an old-fashioned favourite available in a wide range of colours and heights. The La Bella series offers large butterfly or open-faced flowers on bushy plants with strong stems. Available in shades of bronze, lavender, pink, purple, red, white and yellow. "Snaps" make great cutflowers and are definitely child and pet friendly. Height: 50cm; spacing: 25–30cm. Sun.

Sunflower 'Teddy Bear'

Great for children's gardens, this variety of sunflower has a dwarf bushy habit. Orange-gold, 15cm, cuddly, fully double flowers make a good cutflower. Petals are edible. Height: up to 90cm; spacing: 45–60cm. Sun.

Snapdragon 'La Bella Orange Bronze'

Marigold 'Gem Lemon'

Sunflower 'Teddy Bear'

HERBS

Chives
Allium schoenoprasum

This grass-like herb produces attractive spikes of edible foliage and purple flowers that can be used in salads or as garnish. Leaves have a mild onion flavour. Chop leaves and use in recipes or as garnish. Blooms in June. Prefers moderately rich, well-drained soil. Height: 20–60cm; space 30–40cm. Sun to P.M. sun.

Daylily 'El Desperado'

PERENNIALS

Blue Catmint
Nepeta subsessilis

This long-blooming plant brightens up any mixed border with blue-purple flowers from midsummer to fall. Prefers well-drained, moist, cool soil. Clump-forming in habit with aromatic foliage. Height: 60–90cm; width: 30cm. Sun to P.M. sun.

Daylily
Hemerocallis 'El Desperado'

Daylilies are hardy, versatile, clump-forming plants that are not considered poisonous. This variety is an extended bloomer (flowers last longer than a single day). Mustard-yellow blooms with maroon eye and tips appear in late July.

Chives

Ostrich Fern

Prefers moist, fertile, well-drained soil but adapts readily to virtually any type of soil. Height: 70cm; width: 45–75cm. Sun to P.M. sun.

Honeysuckle
Lonicera 'Mandarin'

This attractive climbing vine requires support. Glossy green foliage displays red-orange, sweetly scented, tubular blooms in June. Do not cut back in fall. Height: 3–4m; width: 1–2m. Sun to P.M. sun.

Lemon Beebalm
Monarda punctata

This plant is suitable for the mixed border and attracts bees and hummingbirds. Produces aromatic foliage and purple-spotted, yellow or pink flowers in midsummer to fall. Prefers moist, moderately fertile, well-drained soil. Height: 30–90cm; width: 25–45cm. Sun to P.M. sun.

Ostrich Fern
Matteuccia struthiopteris

This is a very popular, colony-forming native fern with beautiful, arching fronds that resemble ostrich plumes. Requires moist, organic, well-drained, acidic soil. Height: 1–1.5m; width: 60–75cm. Shade to A.M. sun.

TREES & SHRUBS

Cranberry 'Wentworth'
Viburnum trilobum

Great for screening and large shrub beds. Blooms heavily in spring with pretty white clustered flowers followed by high yields of edible and ornamental red fruits that make good juice and jellies. Foliage turns a strong red fall colour. Prefers moist soil. Height: 3–4m; width: 3–4m. Sun to P.M. sun.

Honeysuckle 'Mandarin'

Lemon Beebalm

Cranberry 'Wentworth'

Covering the bare soil with mulch will help discourage cats from using your flowerbeds as litterboxes.

Our yard has several flowerbeds in warm, sunny locations. The problem is that the neighbourhood cats seem to think that these beds are giant litter boxes! I want to find a way to repel cats. What grows here?

CATS JUST LOVE WARM, DRY SOIL in flowerbeds. There are a number of "spray or sprinkle" deterrents on the market and a lot of home-made recipes around, but they all require reapplication after rain or as the scent wears off. Some gardeners report having success with motion detector water sprinklers. Still others swear by spreading used tealeaves, coffee grounds or citrus peels on their beds. We've found one of the simplest and most effective methods of deterring cats is to cover the bare soil in flowerbeds with some kind of mulching material. Cats dislike sharp gravel, pinecones and shredded bark, and these covers are a lot more visually appealing than rotting kitchen scraps in the landscape! There are a number of plants that are said to be repulsive to felines because of scent, including the latest from Germany, *Coleus canina*, which is not yet widely available. You may find that thorny plants offer some relief as well. Cats won't crawl over a prickly pear or barrel cactus to find a litter box, and plants that provide a physical barrier seem more effective than those that repel with their odour. That being said, give one of the plants below a try—you have nothing to lose!

HERBS

Rue
Ruta graveolens
Striking, blue-green, tiny foliage on an upright plant. Blooms June to August. Repels cats. Prefers well-drained soil. Height: 45–90cm. Sun.

PERENNIALS

Blue Sage
Salvia x *sylvestris* 'Blue Hill'
This clump-forming, upright perennial produces very long-lasting blooms that make good cutflowers. Fragrant blue-violet flowers appear in summer. Try cutting back after initial bloom to promote re-blooming. Does best in well-drained, moist, organic soil. Height: 60–75cm; width: 45–60cm wide. Sun to P.M. sun.

Cranesbill
Geranium 'Johnson's Blue'
Perennial geraniums are undemanding and long-lived plants that are suitable as a groundcover for a woodland or shrub bed. Clump-forming in habit with lavender-blue flowers appearing reliably in summer. Does best in well-drained soil. Height: 30–45cm; width: 60–75cm. Sun or shade.

Prickly Thrift
Acantholimon bracteatum
ssp. *capitatum*
This slow-growing but interesting perennial is a favourite in our show garden and resents being moved. It forms a cushion of prickly, evergreen foliage and displays bright pink flowers in summer. Does best in sharply drained, alkaline, dry soil. Height: 10–15cm; width: 10–15cm. Sun.

ROSES

'Charles Albanel' Explorer
Rugosa
This rugged rose makes a stunning groundcover, displaying clusters of large, pretty flowers. Hardy to Zone 1. Semi-double, medium red, 7–9cm flowers bloom all summer. Height: 30–60cm; width: 90cm. Sun.

TREES & SHRUBS

Barberry 'Golden Nugget'
Berberis thunbergii 'Monlers'
A dwarf, slow-growing accent plant that provides contrast in borders, shrub beds and rock gardens. Berries are striking in winter. The newest growth is a deep orange maturing to golden yellow and dense branches have short sharp thorns. Height: 30cm; width: 45cm. Sun.

Blue Sage 'Blue Hill'

Prickly Thrift

Attractive 'Smooth' sumac is a plant that deer will not commonly browse on.

Our half-acre lot is in a lovely country sub-divi-
sion. Over the years we have shared the area with a lot
of wildlife, but now the deer are becoming very bold
and coming right up to the house to eat our foundation
shrubbery! What grows here?

Late one fall, as we harvested the cabbage crop, we scattered
the outer leaves on the snow-covered field next to our vegetable
shed. Not much later, I spotted a solitary deer munching away. After a
couple of weeks of dumping leaves in the field, we soon had thirty deer
feeding in our backyard! Once deer find a safe and consistent food source,
they tend to stick around. As rural areas are developed and natural foods
sources are destroyed, deer will turn (and return) to the tasty plants that
we grow. Some folks hang smelly soaps, sprinkle human hair, or apply
repellants made of coyote or wolf urine around the yard, but these treat-
ments have mixed results. There are a number of plants that deer are less
likely to eat, but if populations are high and food scarce, even these plants
may become a meal. Some people even grow corn or hay specifically for
deer, hoping that offering a tastier meal will keep them from feeding on
ornamental plants, but a barrier, such as a tall fence, is still the best deer
deterrent. And just remember: if you think you've got it bad, I know one
gardener in northern Alberta who has had her garden foraged upon by
not only deer, but elk, moose and even a bison.

ANNUALS

Cleome 'Queen Mix'

A tall, old-fashioned favourite ideally used in backgrounds. Large 12–15cm, spider-like flowers are available in shades of rose, violet, cherry and white. Quite tolerant of heat and drought. Height: up to 1m; spacing: 25–35cm. Sun.

PERENNIALS

Black-Eyed Susan
Rudbeckia hirta

Another old-fashioned favourite that deer don't seem to browse on. Blooms from summer to first frost with golden-yellow flowers with dark brown centres. Use to brighten up a mixed border or as a cutflower. Tolerates poor, dry soils but does best in well-drained, fertile, moist soil. Clump-forming in habit. Height: 60–90cm; width: 30–45cm. Sun to P.M. sun.

Common Foxglove
Digitalis purpurea

Clump-forming and upright in habit, producing flower spikes of yellow, purple, or pink in summer. Allow to self-seed for more plants. Prefers well-drained, fertile, moist soil. Height: 1–2m; width: 60–75cm. Sun to P.M. sun.

Monkshood
Aconitum napellus

This is a poisonous perennial that is unpalatable to mammals. Upright in habit, it produces tall stalks of indigo-blue flowers in late summer. Does best in moist, fertile, cool soil. Height: 90–150cm; width: 30–60cm. Sun to P.M. sun.

TREES & SHRUBS

Pine 'Lodgepole'
Pinus contorta var. *latifolia*

Alberta's provincial tree is hardy and narrow with a beautiful straight trunk. Drought and heat tolerant. Nice planted in groups and good near decks and patios as it doesn't drop cones. Height: 20m; width: 4–6m. Sun.

Sumac 'Smooth'
Rhus glabra

Glossy, smooth bark and tropical-looking leaves make this an interesting plant in the border or used as screening. Both male & female plants are required to produce bright scarlet fruit and plants are sold unsexed, so several must be purchased in hopes of getting both. Greenish-yellow blooms appear in July. Produces striking red fall colour. Requires moist soil. Height: 4–5m; width: 4–5m. Sun to A.M. sun.

Cleome 'Queen Mix'

Monkshood

Salvias, such as those in the Victoria series, are rarely bothered by hungry rabbits.

We have a large rabbit population in our area and, as adorable as these creatures are, they are destroying my flowerbeds. We really don't want to waste any more money on plants that they will eat and want to try plants that are "bunny-resistant." What grows here?

RABBITS CAN BE VORACIOUS, especially in the early spring as tender new shoots come up from the ground or sprout on trees and shrubs. When populations are high or food scarce, rabbits can strip bark from trees and will eat almost anything. You can protect trees and shrubs in winter by caging them with chicken wire or wrapping trunks with protectors. It is a little harder in the warmer months to deter rabbits, as most of us do not want to cage our beds! We've noticed that the plants listed here have been left undisturbed by rabbits in our gardens.

ANNUALS

Salvia (Mealycup Sage), Victoria Series

Narrow spikes of silvery-white and deep violet-blue florets highlight this series, which is a good substitute for lavender. Attracts hummingbirds but not rabbits and makes a good cut or dried flower. Heat tolerant. Height: 45–50cm; Spacing: 25–30cm. Sun.

PERENNIALS

Astilbe
Astilbe japonica 'Deutschland'

Great for a damp woodland or water-side garden, this heavy feeder produces fragrant, white plumes of blooms in summer. Clump-forming habit. Thrives in moist, fertile, organic, alkaline-free soil. Tolerates boggy sites. Height: 45–60cm; width: 40–60cm. Shade to A.M. sun.

Adam's Needle
Yucca filamentosa

Valued for its bold, upright form. Produces dark green, spiky evergreen foliage with curly white threads. White flowers tinged yellow bloom in summer. Does best in a sheltered site away from cold, drying winter winds. Prefers well-drained soil—avoid winter wet. Height: 60–75cm; width: 60–100cm. Sun.

Cushion Spurge
Euphorbia polychroma

This spurge forms a neat mound and never spreads from its allotted space. Bright chartreuse-yellow bracts appear in spring. Tolerant of poor soil but it prefers well-drained, sandy soil in a hot and dry location. Height: 40–60cm; width: 40–60cm. Sun.

Cushion Spurge

Adam's Needle

Astilbe 'Deutschland'

Garden Globeflower
Trollius x *cultorum*

Perfect for moist, woodland gardens, pond sides or shady borders providing globe-shaped, orange-yellow flowers in spring to mid summer. Clump-forming in habit-cut back after flowering for more blooms. Prefers moist, fertile soil. Height: 60–90cm; width: 45cm. Shade to A.M. sun.

Hosta
Hosta 'August Moon'

Handsome and undemanding plants, hostas are quite tolerant of deep shade, but grow best in open shade with dappled sunlight. This variety is clump-forming in habit with broad, golden foliage. Likes slightly acidic, moist, fertile, well-drained soil. Height: 50cm; width: 1m. Shade to A.M. sun.

Lily-of-the-Valley
Convallaria majalis

A vigorous, spreading and dense groundcover for moist or dry areas. Tiny, pendant, bell-shaped, white flowers appear in spring and are fragrant. Attractive orange-red berries follow in fall. Prefers organic, well-drained, moist soil but is tolerant of dry sites. Height: 15–20cm; width: 45–60+cm. Sun or shade.

Plain's Prickly Pear Cactus
Opuntia polyacantha

Native to southern Alberta. In winter, the prickly pads will shrivel up, almost looking dead, as their way of protecting themselves for a cold winter. Plant in a hot, dry site in a rock garden, raised bed, trough or stone wall. Yellow flowers appear in early summer. Requires sharply drained, gritty, moderately fertile soil. Clump-forming and spreading in habit. Height: 8–15cm; width: 30–60+cm. Sun.

Garden Globeflower

Hosta 'August Moon'

Juniper 'Blueberry Delight'

Purple Gas Plant
Dictamnus albus v. *purpureus*

One of the longest living perennials, *Dictamus* produces an abundance of fragrant pink flowers in late spring to early summer. The plants are late to come up in the spring, do not disturb too early. Thrives in dry, moderately fertile, well-drained soil. Clump-forming habit. Height: 75–90cm; width: 60–75cm. Sun to P.M. sun.

TREES & SHRUBS

Juniper 'Blueberry Delight'
Juniperus communis depressa 'Amidak'

This is a dense, wide-spreading groundcover form of juniper that has dark needles with a silver-blue line on upper surface. Use in rock gardens—very hardy. Height: 30cm; width: 150cm. Sun.

Lily-of-the-Valley

Plain's Prickly Pear Cactus

Purple Gas Plant

One of the ways the staff at Butchart Gardens in Victoria, British Columbia, prevent squirrel damage is by covering the bulb beds with large nets.

Last year I planted some tulips to provide early spring co-lour. When none of them came up this year, I realized that squirrels had eaten them. I'd like to plant more and even expand into other bulbs, but I don't want to grow any that will be eaten. What grows here?

SQUIRRELS ARE ATTRACTED TO THE SMELL of certain bulbs and newly disturbed soil. Tulips are a particular favourite. You can coat the bulbs with a repellant at planting time. Some gardeners try using the diversionary tactic of a well-stocked peanut feeder. Mammals won't eat narcissus and, if you interplant them with other bulbs, squirrels may be put off enough to leave your tulips alone! However, laying wire or netting over the beds of edible favourites still seems to be the most foolproof solution; we know of one gardener who uses old screen doors to protect his tulip beds after planting. Chicken wire, used in the same manner, is also very effective. Of course, any physical barrier must be removed in the spring, before the plants emerge!

Fall Bulbs

Allium 'Purple Sensation'
Allium aflatunense

10cm, very dark purple flowers make this variety especially gorgeous—well worth seeking out. One of the hardiest and easiest alliums to grow. Blooms in late spring. Prefers well-drained, sandy soil. Height: 60–90cm; plant 6–10cm deep and 10–12cm apart. Sun.

Colchicum 'Waterlily'
Colchicum

Large, this bulb provides colour in the fall. Leaves appear in early spring and die back before flowers emerge. Double, lilac-pink flowers appear on leafless stems. Plant in a sunny (but not hot), sheltered location. Prefers light, loose, rich soils that are not alkaline. Height: 20cm; plant 10–15cm deep and 15cm apart. Sun.

Winter Aconite
Eranthis cilicica

Blooms in late winter to early spring with 2–3cm, buttercup-like, deep yellow flowers. Naturalizes readily and is best planted in woodland gardens or in borders near deciduous trees or shrubs. Do not fertilize. Provide winter protection. Height: 5–8cm; plant 10–12cm deep, space 5–7cm. P.M. sun or sun (if not hot and dry over summer).

Colchicum 'Waterlily'

Winter Aconite

Allium 'Purple Sensation'

Fritillaria
Fritillaria imperialis 'Lutea'

A striking early to midsummer blooming bulb, displaying a showy cluster
of up to 6 bell-shaped, bright yellow
flowers atop a sturdy stem. It requires
dry conditions for the summer
dormancy period and dislikes being
disturbed once planted. The bulb itself
produces an unpleasant musky odour
that deters rodents and other pests.
Prefers fast-draining soil—water only
when dry. Height: 100–120cm; plant
25–45cm deep to the base of the bulb
and 7–15cm apart. Sun to P.M. sun.

Snowdrop
Galanthus nivalis

Honey-scented, single, pendulous,
bell-shaped, white flowers with green
accents on inner petals appear in very
early spring. This species naturalizes
easily. The most cold-tolerant snow-

drop, disliked by rodents and squirrels.
It requires cool, moist conditions for
the summer dormant period. Prefers
moist, fertile soil. Height: 8–10 cm;
plant 8–10cm deep and 6–8cm apart.
P.M. sun.

Hyacinthoides (Scilla)
Hyacinthoides hispanica

This bulb produces 6–15, bell-shaped
flowers on long, sturdy stems in shades
of blue, pink or white. Blooms in mid
spring and makes a lovely cutflower.
Naturalizes readily and is a good choice
for planting in woodland gardens and
under trees and shrubs. Prefers fertile,
well-drained soil. Height: 25–40cm;
plant 5cm deep and 7–10cm apart. Sun
to P.M. sun.

Fritillaria

Hyacinthoides

Snowdrop

Muscari (Grape Hyacinth)
Muscari azureum

Sweetly scented, open clusters of bell-shaped, sky-blue flowers with a darker stripe bloom in early spring. Plant among later-appearing perennials to help disguise dying foliage. Prefers well-drained soil. Height: 10cm; plant 12–14cm deep and 8cm apart. Sun to P.M. sun.

Narcissus
Narcissus 'Fortissimo'

A large-cupped daffodil with soft yellow flowers with orange cup. Blooms in early spring. Dry, not too hot soil is necessary for the summer dormant period. Recommended for forcing indoors. Height: 30–50cm; 15–20cm deep and 8cm apart. Sun to P.M. sun.

Star of Bethlehem
Ornithogalum

A true bulb that produces white or cream, star-shaped flowers. Blooms in summer to early fall. Use in a perennial garden and as a cutflower. Prefers well-drained soil. Height: 15cm; plant 5–10cm deep and 8–12cm apart. Sun.

Scilla
Scilla siberica

Each bulb produces three to four stems with three to five nodding, bell-shaped, bright true-blue flowers in very early spring. An excellent choice for rock gardens, woodland gardens and in mixed borders. It will not tolerate hot, dry conditions and prefers organic, well-drained, moist soil. Height: 5–10 cm; plant 8cm deep and 4–5cm apart. A.M. or P.M. sun.

Muscari

Scilla

Narcissus 'Fortissimo'

3
Physical Challenges
Living with Limitations

There are any number of physical conditions that can be considered gardening handicaps: allergies, arthritis, blindness and loss of mobility to name a few. We can't deny that physical limitations affect how we live our lives, but it's a mistake to believe that they have to stop us from enjoying the activities we love most in life, including gardening.

I've seen proof of this, over and over, through some of our green-house's best (and most frequent) customers, and the people I've met through my talks. Examples abound. My wife, Marcia, knows of a woman who is a quadriplegic—a woman with "the best garden ever." She researches and chooses the plants she wants and determines where she wants to plant them. She decides what maintenance is required—dividing, fertilizing, pruning—and what steps need to be taken with disease or insect problems. The only thing she doesn't do is the actual physical labour (amending the soil, planting and garden maintenance), which is carried out by her aides, according to her precise instructions. Each year the design is all hers, even though she never lays hands on a single plant.

This woman's methods might not really be all that different from mine, and perhaps even yours. As a professional grower, I have to accept that I can't physically care for every plant singlehandedly, so I manage my resouces—a team of skilled growers who can. A home gardener with any physical handicap faces the task of managing the landscape within the possibilities of that condition. Look at how you can modify your surroundings, and take pride and pleasure in what you *are* able to do.

There are so many ways to enjoy gardening, either on your own or with a little help—so experiment and keep at it! It's the individualized approach that produces the most successful—and satisfying—garden.

IN THE GARDEN

In 1981, avid gardener Viky Gartner lost most of her sight. It hasn't kept her from her love of gardening. In fact, she and her husband, Ed, have an award-winning garden that has been celebrated in local and national publications.

They work together. Ed describes plantings in other gardens, relating colour, form and textural details to Viky. She's responsible for developing their garden's design and records her ideas on tape instead of writing them down. They plant together; Viky tells Ed exactly where everything goes, even going so far as to feel each large rock before it's permanently placed. Ed handles all of the garden's maintenance.

Viky's uncanny sense of proportion, combined with Ed's own insights and labour, has helped them create a stunning yard. Viky enjoys the garden by touch and through Ed's descriptions. "We love it," she says. And that's the only motivation she needs for overcoming her physical challenge. She and Ed are now even helping design and plant their granddaughter's yard!

Raised beds, elevated to a customized height, can eliminate painful bending and kneeling and make gardening more enjoyable.

My husband, who has always been the avid gardener in our family, has developed arthritis and is finding it too difficult to continue with the upkeep of our yard. We are preparing to change the landscape to accommodate his condition, while still allowing him to do what he loves. We want to grow plants that are considered low-maintenance. What grows here?

AVOIDING FUSSY, HIGH–MAINTENANCE plants is an excellent way to reduce yard work, but be also sure to address the specific challenges of any condition that affects range of motion. Raised beds set at a customized height will allow gardening in a seated position, eliminating much of the painful bending associated with traditional beds and borders. Fill the beds with good-quality potting soil—it remains loose and easy to dig in. Lessen the amount of work even more by planting thickly or using mulch on the beds (both help to keep weeds down and soil moist). Choose garden tools that are easy to use and look for long-handled trowels and forks. You may opt to fill these beds completely with quick-growing annuals or a combination of plants that are neat and compact, requiring very little in the way of pruning, and that are disease and pest resistant as well.

ANNUALS

Calibrachoa, Million Bells Series

A fast-growing, heavy-blooming and self-cleaning plant that thrives in hanging baskets, containers or grown as an annual groundcover. Produces small, petunia-like blooms in many colourful shades. Height: 8–15cm; trails to 60cm. Sun.

Lavatera 'Silver Cup'

These bushy plants produce satiny rose, cup-shaped flowers—very showy in the garden. Great in mass displays. Wind tolerant. Height: 60–90cm; spacing: 40–60cm. Sun.

Petunia, Easy Wave Series

A really versatile petunia that has a spreading and mounded growth habit. Excellent in hanging baskets, patio pots or raised beds. Bright, 6cm, weather-tolerant flowers bloom all summer. Height: 20–30cm; spreads to 75cm. Sun to P.M. sun.

Calibrachoa 'Million Bells Cherry Pink'

Petunia 'Easy Wave Cherry'

Lavatera 'Silver Cup'

PERENNIALS

Asiatic Lily
Lilium 'Avignon'

Asiatic lilies are unmatched for wonderful blooms in the summer perennial bed. These clump-forming plants
are pest resistant and hardy, producing
blooms that make excellent cutflowers.
'Avignon' produces soft orange-red
flowers in early summer. Prefers fertile,
well-drained, organic soil. Height: 1m;
width: 30–45cm. Sun to P.M. sun.

Daylily
Hemerocallis 'Little Grapette'

A shorter daylily for the front border
which produces red-purple flowers in
June. Divide every three to five years to
maintain vigour. Prefers moist, fertile,
well-drained soil. Clump-forming in
habit. Height: 30cm; wide: 30–60cm.
Sun.

Peony
Paeonia 'Festiva Supreme'

Peonies are great low-maintenance,
clump-forming plants. They are hardy,
pest and disease-resistant and vigorous.
'Festiva Supreme' displays fragrant, fully
double, white flowers in late spring that
make excellent cutflowers. Peonies enjoy moist, acid-free, fertile, well-drained
soil. Height: 1m; width: 90–100cm. Sun
to P.M. sun.

Peony 'Festiva Supreme'

Daylily 'Little Grapette'

Asiatic Lily 'Avignon'

Trees & Shrubs

Cranberry 'Alfredo Compact'
Viburnum trilobum

An ideal, easy shrub for hedging or borders. This extremely compact plant has very dense foliage turning a striking red fall colour. Produces bright red, edible fruits. Height: 1.5–2m; width: 1.5–2m. Sun to P.M. sun.

Juniper 'Blue Star'
Juniperus squamata

Very bright blue foliage on a slow-growing, rounded bush that does not require pruning to maintain its attractive form. Best with good snowcover through winter. Height: 90cm; width: 1–1.5m. Sun.

Lilac 'Miss Kim'
Syringa patula

A non-suckering, dwarf variety whose foliage turns purple in fall. Icy lilac-purple, very fragrant blooms open in early summer. Height: 90–150cm; width: 90–150cm. Sun to P.M. sun.

Pine 'Mops'
Pinus mugo

An ideal small pine for small shrub beds that is very heat tolerant. Naturally dense in habit and slow-growing—doesn't need pruning to maintain shape. Height: 1m; width: 1m in 15–18 years. Sun to P.M. sun.

Pine 'Mops'

Lilac 'Miss Kim'

Juniper 'Blue Star'

The beautiful CNIB gardens in Calgary, Alberta are designed to engage all of the senses.

I'm interested in planting a garden for my daughter, who is visually impaired. I've done some reading about one planted specifically for the blind at the Canadian National Institute for the Blind (CNIB) in Calgary, Alberta. I'd like to incorporate some of their ideas and plant selections into our garden. What grows here?

THE GARDEN TO WHICH YOU REFER is planned to allow visually impaired people (who, more often than not, are not completely blind) to engage all of their senses in enjoying the landscape. Taste, smell, sound, touch and yes, even *sight* should be considered and accounted for in a garden plan. Plant blocks of brightly coloured plants that have strong visual impact, and select plants based upon their other sensual characteristics with particular emphasis placed on fragrance. Safety is also a priority with the use of clearly defined borders and flat, firm paths, as well as audible clues, like wind chimes or gurgling water features installed at entrances and exits. Plants that have sharp thorns are not recommended and wayward branches should be kept pruned back. It's important to note that individuals with other special needs (such as those with autism and even Alzheimer's) also appreciate gardens planned with all the senses in mind.

ANNUALS

Heliotrope 'Marine Blue'

Heliotrope's clustered blooms offer texture, strong fragrance and deep purple colour. The striking blooms attract hummingbirds. Great in patio pots and planters. Height: 35cm; spacing: 25–30cm. Sun.

Marigold, Bonanza Series

Create wide swaths of strong colour with these marigolds in shades ranging from deep bronze to bright yellow. The large, 5cm, double flowers are showy in mass displays, containers and borders. A very heat-tolerant plant. Height: 20cm; spacing: 15–20cm. Sun to P.M. sun.

Sunflower 'Ballad'

This dwarf sunflower is just the right height to be appreciated by a child and features bright, golden-yellow flower petals with a dark centre. Ballad's shiny green foliage is mildew tolerant and its blooms have no pollen. Good cutflower. Height: up to 60cm; spacing: 45–60cm. Sun.

Sweet Pea, Cuthbertson Floribunda Series

Grow these fragrant beauties up a fence or along railings. Lots of sweetly-scented, long-stemmed flowers in nice shades. Great cutflowers. Strong climbing habit. Height: up to 2m; spacing: 10–20cm. Sun.

Sunflower 'Ballad'

Marigold 'Bonanza Mix'

Heliotrope 'Marine Blue'

Beebalm
Monarda 'Marshall's Delight'

A clump-forming plant suitable for the mixed border and attractive to bees and hummingbirds. Produces aromatic foliage and is long-blooming with large, rose-pink flowers in summer. This variety is highly mildew-resistant. Does best in moist, moderately fertile, well-drained soil. Height: 60–90cm; width: 45–60cm. Sun to P.M. sun.

Lamb's Ears
Stachys byzantina

This perennial is grown for its silver-grey, woolly foliage (the small purple flowers that appear in summer are often removed as the stems tend to flop over). Excellent for edging forming a thick, spreading groundcover. Prefers fertile, well-drained soil but adapts well to dry sites. Height: 45–60cm; width: 45–60+cm. Sun to P.M. sun.

True Lavender
Lavandula angustifolia 'Munstead'

This is a compact, early-flowering variety that is one of the hardiest lavenders. Fragrant blooms make excellent dried potpourri. Plant on the west or south side of a warm wall or fence and do not cut back. Mulch in winter. Requires moderately fertile, well-drained soil. Height: 30–45cm; width: 45–60cm. Sun to P.M. sun.

Beebalm 'Marshall's Delight'

Lamb's Ears

Roses

'J.P. Connell' Explorer
Hardy Shrub

This is the most fragrant rose of the Explorer series. Hardy to Zone 3, it blooms singly or in clusters of double, creamy-yellow, 7–9cm flowers with a light 'Tea' fragrance. Blooms appear repeatedly from early summer to frost. Height: 60–90cm; width: 60–90cm. Sun.

Trees & Shrubs

Daphne 'Rose'
Daphne cneorum

Daphne offers dark green foliage on a dense form with clusters of rose-pink, very fragrant blooms in May. It may re-bloom in late summer. Light sun is best; keep well-watered in sunny sites. Requires snow cover for best results. Shear and shape after flowering. Height: 15–30cm Width: 60–90cm. A.M. sun.

Lilac 'Mount Baker'
Syringa x *hyacinthiflora*

This lilac offers height to the garden providing masses of white, fragrant, single blooms in spring and a dark green solid background the rest of the growing season. An excellent choice for large shrub beds as it's non-suckering. Height: 3–4m; width: 3–4m. Sun to P.M. sun.

Daphne 'Rose'

'J.P. Connell' Rose

Lilac 'Mount Baker'

Only the single flowers of the Non-Stop series begonias produce pollen, so simply pinch them off and enjoy the double, pollen-free blooms instead.

I have developed terrible allergies over the years and as a result had given up entirely on gardening. A friend recently told me that there actually are allergen-free plants that I could use in my garden and still have colour. What grows here?

THERE REALLY ARE NO *completely* allergen-free plants; however, there are many low-allergen plants. The issue is complicated because reactions to allergens are extremely individual and often based upon the quantity of exposure. Of the common allergens encountered in the garden, pollen and dust are found in the greatest quantity. Plants with sterile flowers are less likely to trigger allergic reactions. Plants pollinated by insects have relatively small quantities of sticky, heavy pollen in comparison with plants (such as grasses) that rely on air currents to distribute their light, abundant pollen. Furry foliage may not cause a pollen reaction, but textured leaves that trap dust can. Be careful using compost and organic mulches. They are rich in spores that you may react to—use groundcover plants instead. If your allergies are severe, avoid gardening on damp, hot and still days. Instead, enjoy your garden on cool and slightly breezy days.

ANNUALS

Begonia, Non-Stop Series

Non-Stop begonias produce both single and double flowers on a single plant. The single blooms produce pollen, so simply pinch them off and leave the pretty, double blooms to provide colour. The Non-Stop series produces large, double flowers in bright clear colours. Mounding habit is excellent in hanging baskets, containers, flowerbeds. Height: 20–25cm; spacing: 15–25cm. Shade to A.M. sun.

FRUIT

Cherry 'Nanking'
Prunus

This is a versatile cherry often used as an ornamental for hedges or trained to small tree form. Pretty pink blooms in early spring are followed by 4–11kg yields of 2cm, sweet cherries. Use for pies, jellies or enjoy eating fresh. Height: 2–3m; spreads; 2–3m. Sun.

PERENNIALS

Big Petal Clematis
Clematis macropetala 'Markham's Pink' *(C. macropetala* v. *markhami)*

Produces a lush, pest-free and very hardy screen that requires support. Grow as a climber, groundcover or trailing over stone walls. Do not cut back. Pink-mauve flowers in spring are followed by atractive seed heads. Prefers fertile, well-drained soil and cool roots. Height: 3–5 m; width: 75–90cm. Sun to P.M. sun.

Peony 'Milton Jack'

Carpathian Bellflower
Campanula carpatica 'White Clips'

This clump-forming perennial has a compact habit that displays its blooms well. Bell-shaped, white flowers appear in summer. Prefers moist, fertile, well-drained soil for best flower display. Height: 20–25cm; width: 30cm. Sun to P.M. sun.

Peony
Paeonia 'Milton Jack'

Peonies are clump-forming, slow-growing but long-lived perennials. Their fragrant blooms can be enjoyed indoors. 'Milton Jack' produces striking, double, dark rose-red flowers in spring. Prefers moist, acid-free, fertile, well-drained soil. Height: 90cm; width: 90cm–1m. Sun to P.M. sun.

TREES & SHRUBS

Fir 'Dwarf Balsam'
Abies balsamea 'Nana'

A really nice addition to a mixed border or rock garden. This dwarf form displays dark green, broad and flat needles. Prefers moist soil. Height: 60–75cm; width: 100cm. A.M. sun.

Fir 'Dwarf Balsam'

In cold climates the width and soil volume of raised beds will be one of the factors that determines which plants over-winter in them.

I am in the process of designing a garden that will allow full access in my wheelchair. All of the beds will be raised to a height and width that work best for me. I need hardy plants that will over-winter in these beds. What grows here?

RAISED BEDS OFFER A LOT of advantages for every gardener—even those without mobility issues. Plants are often more fully appreciated when they are displayed in a raised bed; smaller plants tend to look more substantial. The width and depth of the beds you design will dictate which perennials, shrubs and perhaps, depending on the harshness of winters in your area, even small trees you can over-winter. You can make the beds wider, increasing the soil volume to protect plant roots from the bitter cold, as long as you can garden from both sides of the bed. Think beyond raised beds in your design by hanging baskets on a pulley system or mounting them on shepherd's hooks. The task of watering can be simplified by investing in a hose for each area, installing soaker hoses or irrigation systems in the beds, and using a long-handled watering wand. Thoughtful landscape design that includes raised beds is just one way of making gardening possible for every body.

PERENNIALS

Coralbells
Heuchera sanguinea 'Morden Pink'

A hardy plant with attractive foliage and tiny pink blooms, held atop the foliage on stalks in late spring to early summer. May require replanting every two years in fall, as crowns tend to push upwards. Requires moist, fertile, well-drained soil. Height: 45–60cm; width: 30cm. Sun to P.M. sun.

White Sage
Salvia x *sylvestris* 'Snow Hill'

This clump-forming salvia offers upright stalks of pure white flowers in summer. Good cutflower. Cut back after flowering to promote re-blooming. Prefers well-drained, moist, organic soil. Height: 30–45cm; width: 45–60cm. Sun to P.M. sun.

ROSES

'Scarlet Pavement' Pavement
Hardy Shrub

A tough rugosa hybrid that has a low, sprawling habit—attractive spilling over retaining wall edges. Produces semi-double, fuchsia-red to light red, 6–8cm flowers all summer and forms dark red rosehips in fall. Height: 90cm; width: 100cm. Sun.

TREES & SHRUBS

Falsecypress 'Sungold'
Chamaecyparis pisifera

A really pretty, low-maintenance addition to a large raised bed in an area sheltered from drying winter winds. New growth is a very bright yellow and the foliage is dense and thread-like. Great for contrast. Height: 2–3m; width: 2–3m. Sun.

Pine 'Hillside Creeper'
Pinus sylvestris

A great feature grown around rocks and spilling over walls. Fast-growing form used as a groundcover with no pruning maintenance required. Height: 30–60cm; width: 2–3m. Sun.

Spiraea 'Fritschiana'
Spiraea fritschiana

This spiraea is spectacular both in bloom and in full fall colour. Bright white blooms in early summer cover the compact, mounding form for several weeks. Prune after blooming. Height: 60–90cm; width: 75–100cm. Sun to P.M. sun.

Spiraea 'Fritschiana'

White Sage 'Snow Hill'

4
Living with Big Trees

Giants in the Garden

I love big trees—maples in particular. They provide shade, serenity, incredible fall colour, gorgeous bark…and they're a great climbing tree. When my favourite maple was seriously injured during a storm, I went to great lengths to save it by literally bolting the split branch back onto the trunk. Thirty years later, you can still see my repair job, now nearly overgrown with new wood. Was it worth the trouble? Definitely.

That's not to say that gardening with big trees doesn't have its challenges, however it's not always easy to grow plants underneath a shady canopy or for small plants to compete with giant trees for ground moisture. You have to be willing to compromise to keep both. Yes, sometimes a tree must be removed (especially when it becomes unsafe), but more often than not, pruning judiciously and using the right plants to work with the existing conditions makes the most sense. (Don't give up hope of ever having an attractive yard that includes a diverse collection of plants.)

If you're just starting out, or are replacing or adding a tree to your landscape, avoid the common mistake of choosing a "pretty little tree" that quickly grows into an unmanageable monster. A sugar maple, for example, may seem like a great choice initially, but will outgrow a small yard in no time, blocking sunlight, growing into power lines and branching into neighbouring yards. In fact, several of the popular maples—sugar, silver, big leaf and Norway, for example—are far too big for all but the largest yards. When space is limited, choose smaller, compact maples such as amur, Japanese or tatarian.

I'll never lose my fondness for towering, magnificent trees, and I know that millions of people feel the same way. These giants not only provide a lifetime's worth of beauty but leave a legacy for generations to come. I think that inheritance is worth a little extra work.

IN THE GARDEN

Tim Morrison and Roxeanne Bunyan's tree-filled yard was a difficult place to successfully garden.

Many large trees cast shade, monopolized soil moisture and, in the case of the spruce and pine trees, dropped loads of needles. But the trees cooled the house and made it possible to enjoy the south-facing backyard in the heat of summer.

Tim evaluated the trees' location, size and health, and removed the most troublesome and least healthy. He then worked the remaining trees into his plans. He started by pruning off dead branches, instantly improving the garden's look. Then he pruned a little more, to allow more light into the yard. In some cases, Tim removed several lower branches and created interesting beds beneath the tree canopies and beyond. The plants he selected to fill these beds were tough, hardy and drought tolerant.

Tim and Roxeanne's renovated garden has an intimate, but not claustrophobic, Asian feel—something they couldn't have achieved if he'd removed all of the trees. In this case, compromise made all the difference.

Even though prominent roots in the lawn may be quite difficult to mow around, do not remove them.

We have large trees in our front yard whose roots get in the way of mowing the lawn. My husband would like either to remove the roots or dig out the lawn around the trees and make a flowerbed. What grows here?

TREE ROOTS ARE, by and large, rather lazy. They are not the great underground explorers that we often imagine, plunging deep into the earth in search of water and nutrients. In reality, they proliferate where the living is easy, near the soil surface, where air, moisture and nutrients are abundant. If your tree is producing surface roots, it means there is probably only a thin layer of soil to support the tree. The soil beneath is likely compacted clay (hostile territory that is impenetrable to tree roots). Surface rooting in lawn areas is bothersome, but the above-ground parts of a plant depend upon the roots for anchorage, absorption of water, minerals and nutrients, storage of food reserves, and synthesis of certain organic materials. We do not recommend removing the roots as a common practice—the results could potentially be disastrous. You can strip the sod, working carefully around tree roots, and make a shallow flowerbed in which to grow plants (provided they receive adequate moisture and light). As a rough rule, do not add more than 5–6 centimetres of soil to the area under the tree, as doing so can deprive the roots of oxygen. Roots without adequate oxygen will quickly die.

ANNUALS

Begonia, Non-Stop Series

This series offers non-stop colour with large, double flowers displayed on a plant with a mounding habit. Excellent in hanging baskets, containers and flowerbeds. Height: 20–25cm; spacing: 15–25cm. Shade to A.M. sun.

Impatiens, Fiesta Series

Superb feature plants in hanging baskets, containers or flowerbeds. Produces fully double, rose-like blooms in many shades on a compact, mounding form. Height: 25–30cm; spacing: 15–20cm. Sun.

FRUIT

Raspberry 'Arctic Groundcover'
Rubus arcticus

A great novelty groundcover offering blooms and fall foliage colour. Pink-purple flowers in early spring develop into small, fire-engine red fruits with wonderful flavour in summer. Light yields in the first year. Height: 8cm; spread: 30cm. Sun to A.M. sun.

Raspberry 'Arctic Groundcover'

PERENNIALS

Japanese Spurge
Pachysandra terminalis

An attractive, dense-carpeting ground-cover for damp, shady areas. Produces glossy, evergreen foliage and spiked, white flowers in early summer. Prefers moist soil. Do not cut back in fall. Height: 15–20cm; width: 60–90+cm. Shade to A.M. sun.

White Archangel
Lamium maculatum
'Purple Dragon'

Makes a wonderful groundcover for shady sites but is tolerant of sun and poor soils. Displays deep purple flowers in spring to summer and silver and green foliage. Prefers well-drained, moist soil. Spreading habit. Height: 10–25cm; width: 60cm–1m. Shade to A.M. sun.

Wild Columbine
Aquilegia canadensis

A clump-forming, native wildflower; perfect for a natural, wild garden. Will tolerate considerable shade. Good flower for attracting hummingbirds. Will freely self-sow. Yellow and red flowers appear in spring. Prefers fertile, well-drained, moist soil. Height: 30–40cm; width: 20–30cm. Sun to P.M. sun.

Begonia 'Non-Stop Rose Petticoat'

Select trees whose mature size fits your yard and plant them as far away from paths and driveways as possible.

At our last home, we battled with the roots of trees crossing the lawn and even lifting and cracking the concrete sidewalk. Now that we have moved and are about to begin landscaping our new yard, we'd like to choose trees that don't present root problems. What grows here?

THE ROOTS OF SOME TREES can extend laterally for quite a distance, and the pressure that large roots place on pavement can eventually cause cracking (which is then penetrated by finer roots). We create a problem when we try to squeeze large trees into small yards, or grow them too close to sidewalks or driveways. The development, size and form of root systems are controlled by the genetic makeup of a plant and its growing environment. It's a common myth that some trees have a single deep taproot, but research has shown that to be a fallacy. Trying to select a tree based on this misconception is fruitless. Instead, choose a tree based on the size of your yard and the tree's mature canopy spread—and place it as far away from paths and driveways as possible. Plant trees in the right location, in good soil, and maintain them by watering, fertilizing and protecting them from damage.

Black Walnut
Juglans nigra

A beautiful, long-lived feature tree displaying coarse, fern-like foliage on a very large, round-headed form. Use in large yards. Does best in deep, rich soil. Height: 15–25m; width: 10–15m. Sun.

Butternut
Juglans cinerea

This hardy tree has a tropical appearance and produces large, edible nuts that are sweet and oily. Long, lacy leaves are attractive. Grows slowly in heavy soil. Blooms in June. Does best in a wind protected site. Height: 12–15m; width: 9–12m. Sun.

Hazelnut 'American'
Corylus americana

A large shrub native to North America. Grow singly or use in groups for screens, informal hedges or for naturalizing. Produces showy spring catkins and edible nuts that mature in the fall, attracting birds and squirrels. Height: 3–5m; width: 2–3m. Sun to P.M. sun.

Hazelnut 'American'

Black Walnut

Butternut

Honeylocust 'Prairie Silk'

Gleditsia triacanthos var. *inermis*

An open-headed tree that provides dappled shade. A great substitute for Elm. Produces fragrant blooms in June and lacy foliage with clear yellow fall colour. Height: 10m; width: 10m. Sun.

Horse Chestnut

Aesculus hippocastanum

An excellent shade tree for large yards. Pointed clusters of white blooms appear in May/June on a large, dense, round-headed form. Height: 10–15m; width: 10–15m. Sun to P.M. sun.

Linden 'Morden Little-leaf'

Tilia cordata 'Morden'

A slower-growing tree, great in smaller yards. Has a straight steel-grey coloured trunk and a nice narrow, upright, oval form. Fragrant yellow flowers appear in June/July. Height: 10m; width: 8m. Sun.

Mountain Ash 'European'

Sorbus aucuparia

This tree provides landscape interest all year. White flowers bloom in spring followed by clusters of orange-red fruit and stunning yellow-orange-red fall colour. A lovely oval, upright form that is great in small yards. Available as a single or multi-stemmed form. Prefers well-drained soil. Height: 7–10m; width: 5–7m. Sun.

Linden 'Morden Little-leaf'

Honeylocust 'Prairie Silk'

Mountain Ash 'European'

Oak 'Burr'

Quercus macrocarpa

Oaks should be thought of as 'heritage' trees and planted where they can be enjoyed for generations to come. This form has a wide, pyramidal shape and offers stunning fall colour. Slow-growing and hardy, well suited to large yards. Prefers acidic soil. Height: 20–25m; width: 9–10m. Sun.

Oak 'Northern Pin'

Quercus ellipsoidalis

Another nice oak, 'Northern Pin' is a bit faster growing than 'Burr' Oak. It displays glossy summer foliage followed by striking russet-red foliage in fall. A hardy selection for northern areas. Height: 15–20m; width: 10m. Sun.

Serviceberry 'Autumn Brilliance'

Amelanchier x *grandiflora*

Serviceberry displays pretty pinkish-white blooms in spring and incredible red fall colour. This tree makes a very nice feature in a small yard. Avoid windy sites. Height: 6–7m; width: 4–6m. Sun to P.M. sun.

Serviceberry 'Autumn Brilliance'

Oak 'Northern Pin'

Oak 'Burr'

Lilacs can be used as hedging, but be sure to select a variety that doesn't spread by sending out suckers.

I have recently moved into an older home where the yard is surrounded by overgrown lilac hedges. They are sending up shoots in the lawn. I'm considering ripping them out, even though I love their blooms and fragrance. I'd still like to have a hedge. What grows here?

OFTEN PLANTS ARE CONSIDERED good hedging material exactly because of their suckering tendencies. They spread, growing into each other to form a solid wall of growth. Unfortunately, as they continue growing and spreading, they don't stay in tidy rows. It's not easy to control the direction in which the roots spread on such plants unless you are prepared to install a barrier. One of our customers planted a hedge along his driveway and then sunk a barrier, effectively forming an open-bottomed trench that stopped roots from spreading. Alternatively, use plants that don't sucker and are used less commonly used for hedging. Consider the purpose of the hedge (privacy or border definition). Given the wide range of plants that can be used, a hedge can have many different looks; it doesn't have to be a solid wall of foliage. Have a vision of the type of hedge you want: manicured and formal, or an informal, loose row of shrubs. And you don't have to give up on lilacs completely—there are several varieties that do not sucker.

ANNUALS

Kochia 'Childsii'

This plant has a uniformly bushy
growth habit that makes an interesting
annual hedge that turns brilliant red in
fall. Soft, feathery, bright green foliage
covers the oval form. Heat and drought
tolerant. Height: 60–90cm; spacing:
30cm. Sun.

TREES & SHRUBS

Cedar 'Brandon'
Thuja occidentalis

Medium to dark green, dense foliage
on an upright form of cedar. Use as
a feature, singly or grouped. Makes a
striking screen or hedge. Best grown
in a moist, humid site. Height: 9–10m;
width: 2–3m. Sun to P.M. sun.

Cedar 'Techny' (Mission)
Thuja occidentalis

This hardy, slow-growing cedar makes
a very attractive, dense living fence that
is wind tolerant. Its dark green foliage,
which looks coarse when young, is
very tolerant of shearing and shaping.
Height: 3–5m; width: 2m. Sun to P.M.
sun.

Kochia 'Childsii'

Nannyberry

Lilac 'Dwarf Korean'
Syringa meyeri 'Palibin'

A dwarf form of lilac that makes a
lovely hedge. Late each spring red-
purple buds open to pink-purple,
fragrant blooms on a non-suckering
and compact plant. Height: 1–2 m;
width: 1.5–2m. Sun to P.M. sun.

Nannyberry
Viburnum lentago

This shrub produces lustrous, compact,
dark green foliage and creamy-white
blooms in June followed by edible,
blue-black fruits. Fruits are excellent
for jams and jellies. Prune after flowering. Height: 4–5m; width: 2–3m. Sun
or shade.

Ninebark 'Diabolo'
Physocarpus opulifolius

A versatile and useful shrub for large
shrub beds or as an informal hedge. It
offers super contrast with rich purple
foliage on strong, upright branches.
Really attractive, pink clustered blooms
appear in summer, followed by interesting pink seed heads. Height: 2–3m;
width: 2–3m. Sun to P.M. sun.

Ninebark 'Diabolo'

Big trees cast shade and take up lots of moisture, making gardening beneath them quite a challenge.

Our neighbour's big trees cast shade on our yard most of the day. We get only morning light and have trouble growing many plants in the dry soil. We would really like some blooms and interesting foliage. What grows here?

SHADE AND DRY SOIL are two problems that when presented in combination, can be quite challenging. Limited light prevents many plants from reaching their full blooming potential and lack of moisture discourages growth. If these trees were on your property, you could re-move some and prune others to allow more light to come through. Ask your neighbour about such a possibility, perhaps even offering to share the costs of having an arborist do the work. If that's not possibile, take a close look at drought- and shade-tolerant groundcovers, and consider using containers of colourful, blooming shade annuals. Amend the soil in your yard to include organic matter and mulch the beds to help retain moisture, but be prepared to continue to water frequently.

ANNUALS

Coleus, Kong Series

A new series of coleus featuring five different varieties, each with large, 20–25cm leaves in a kaleidoscope of interesting colour blends. Use in containers for great contrast—really impressive. Prefers moist, well-drained, fertile, organic soil. Height: 45–50cm; spacing: 30cm. Shade to A.M. sun.

Cosmos 'Cosmic Orange'
C. sulphureus

There are very few drought and shade-tolerant annuals, but this variety of cosmos, considered heat and drought tolerant, has shown ability to grow in less light. Bright orange, 5cm, semi-double flowers make great cutflowers. Excellent in mass displays or borders. Height: 30cm; spacing: 20cm. Sun to P.M. sun.

PERENNIALS

Bethlehem Sage
Pulmonaria saccharata

Pulmonarias are very tough, clump-forming plants that are well suited as groundcovers for a woodland or border edging. Blue flowers appear in spring but these plants are prized for their spotted foliage. Prefers fertile, well-drained, organic soil but will tolerate poor soil. Height: 20–30cm; width: 45–60cm. Shade to A.M. sun.

Heartleaf Bergenia
Bergenia cordifolia

This versatile perennial grows in a wide range of soil and moisture conditions. Glossy, evergreen foliage tints purple in winter and pale to dark pink flowers bloom in spring. Do not cut back in fall. Clump-forming in habit. Height: 40–45cm; wide: 60cm. Sun or shade.

Cosmos 'Cosmic Orange'

Bethlehem Sage

Coleus, Kong Series

Japanese Spurge
Pachysandra terminalis

An attractive, dense-carpeting ground-cover for shady areas. Produces glossy, evergreen foliage and spiked, white flowers in early summer. Prefers moist soil, but is tolerant of dry conditions. Do not cut back in fall. Height: 15–20cm; width: 60–90+cm. Shade to A.M. sun.

Saxifrage
Saxifraga bronchialis

A clump-forming plant with evergreen foliage. Produces soft yellow flowers in spring. Prefers fertile, well-drained, moist soil. Height: 5–10cm; width: 15cm. Sun to P.M. sun.

Lady's Mantle
Alchemilla mollis

This plant is a lovely addition to the garden. It produces lots of long-lasting, lime-green flowers from late spring to fall that make great cutflowers. Its slightly lobed leaves look especially pretty after rain. Prefers well-drained soil but adapts to drier conditions. Clump-forming in habit. Height: 45cm; width: 45cm. Sun to P.M. sun.

Lady's Mantle

Japanese Spurge

Red Barrenwort

Epimedium x *rubrum*

Makes a delightful groundcover for difficult areas. Displays ruby-red flowers in spring and young foliage that is tinted red. The foliage reddens again in fall. Prefers organic, well-drained, moist soil, but grows well in drier conditions. Clump-forming in habit. Height: 25–40cm; width: 30–45cm. Shade to A.M. sun.

Sweet Woodruff

Galium odoratum

Use as a groundcover in cool, shady gardens or beneath trees or shrubs. Its foliage is hay-scented when dried. Blooms in spring to midsummer, displaying fragrant white flowers. Prefers moist, organic soil but is quite tolerant of drier conditions. Creeping in habit. Height: 15–45cm; width: 30+cm. Shade to A.M. sun.

TREES & SHRUBS

Potentilla 'Nuuk'

Potentilla tridentata

This plant hails from Greenland and is useful in shrub beds as an attractive, spreading evergreen groundcover. White blooms appear in June and sporadically through summer. Tolerant of dry soil and lower light conditions. Height: 8–10cm; width: 30–45cm. Sun to P.M. sun.

Potentilla 'Nuuk'

Sweet Woodruff

Red Barrenwort

Prune large trees to improve their form, maintain health and allow more light into a yard.

I have a very small backyard containing a single tree, planted squarely in the yard's center, which casts a lot of shade. The area beneath and around it is moist but I'm having some trouble growing anything in the tree's shadow. I love flowers and would really like to grow some in my yard. What grows here?

THERE ARE A LIMITED NUMBER of plants that will bloom in a fully shaded location. Anything you can do to increase light levels even a little will increase the number of plants from which to choose. Observe the tree carefully, and consider consulting a certified arborist. Can the tree be pruned to allow a little more sunlight into the garden while improving its form and making it a truly beautiful landscape feature? Paint fences and structures white and use light-coloured rock in your scheme to reflect as much light as possible. If you choose plants with white, yellow or other light shades of blooms or foliage, you'll find that they really stand out in shaded areas. Create a focal point, be it a birdbath, statue or bench, and surround it with plants to finish the area off.

ANNUALS

Impatiens, Dazzler Series

Impatiens are the annual workhorses of the shade garden, providing consistent bright colour to dark areas. This series displays masses of 4cm, single flowers in many shades. Height: 20–25cm; spacing: 10–15cm. Shade to A.M. sun.

PERENNIALS

Hosta
Hosta 'Patriot'

Grown for its attractive clumping form and dark green foliage with white margins. Produces lavender blooms in summer. Prefers moist, fertile, well-drained, organic, slightly acidic soil. Height: 60cm; width: 1m. Shade to A.M. sun.

Goldleaf Bleeding Heart
Dicentra spectabilis 'Goldheart'

A pretty groundcover in a woodland garden with striking lime-green foliage. It will go dormant in sunny hot locations. Produces pink flowers in spring to early summer and prefers moist, well-drained, fertile, organic soil. Height: 75–90cm; width: 75–90cm. Shade to A.M. sun.

Rayflower
Ligularia japonica

Deeply-cut, large leaves and clustered, daisy-like, yellow-orange flowers in early summer—a tropical look for the shade garden. Avoid bright, windy sites. Prefers very, moist, deep, moderately fertile soil. Clump-forming and upright in habit. Height: 1–1.5m; width: 75–100cm. Shade to A.M. sun.

TREES & SHRUBS

Dogwood 'Siberian Pearls'
Cornus alba

This shrub provides interest throughout the year. Creamy-white blooms in spring are followed by masses of pearly-white berries. Dark green foliage turns a rich reddish-purple in fall and in winter its red stems are visible. Height: 2–3m; width: 2–3m. Sun to P.M. sun.

Ninebark 'Tilden Parks'
Physocarpus opulifolius

Prized for its ability to grow in shade—a dense, fast-growing groundcover that few weeds can grow through. Great for erosion control on slopes. Produces small, white blooms in spring. Height: 40–50cm; width: 60–100cm. Sun or shade.

Dogwood 'Siberian Pearls'

Impatiens 'Dazzler Deep Pink'

A large poplar can transpire anywhere from 500 to 2,500 litres of water on a warm, sunny day leaving very little moisture in the surrounding soil for other plants, including grass.

There are huge poplars growing in my neighbour's yard and as a result the grass in my yard is dying. Fortunately, these trees don't cast shade onto my property, so there is still lots of light, but very little moisture. What grows here?

LARGE TREES LIFT ENORMOUS AMOUNTS of water from the soil; it's been estimated that a large poplar can transpire anywhere from 500 to 2,500 litres of water on a warm, sunny day. That doesn't leave a lot of left-over moisture for any plants that lie in the path of its roots. The more trees you have, the greater the scope of the problem. One of our customers faced this problem and we suggested she change the style of her garden. Her English cottage garden required vigilant watering—almost every day. We explained some principles of xeriscape (low-water) design and then walked her through our show garden. One of the most popular features there is a lovely rock garden filled with drought-tolerant plants. She went home and began implementing a new plan. When the neighbour with the offending trees asked what she was up to, she explained the situation. It turned out that he had wanted to re-landscape and only needed to see what she was doing to be inspired. He promptly had a tree service remove some of the poplars, leaving just a few for shade, and started working on his own yard.

PERENNIALS

Common Beardtongue
Penstemon barbatus ssp. *coccineus* 'Rondo'

Penstemon is quite tolerant of dry conditions. Use in any mixed border where in summer their attractive red flowers, tinted pink to carmine, attract hummingbirds. Prefers fertile, well-drained soil. Upright in habit. Height: 50–90cm; width: 30–45cm. Sun to P.M. sun.

False Sunflower
Heliopsis 'Loraine Sunshine'

Green and white variegated foliage makes this a great contrast plant suited for any mixed border. Golden-yellow flowers bloom midsummer to fall and make excellent cutflowers. Prefers fertile, well-drained, moist, organic soil but is quite heat and drought tolerant. Clump-forming in habit. Height: 60–90cm; width: 30–45cm. Sun to P.M. sun.

TREES & SHRUBS

Barberry 'Rose Glow'
Berberis thunbergii var. *atropurpurea*

Extremely tolerant of heat, this barberry is especially striking planted en masse or used as a contrast shrub. Yellow blooms appear in May and June and are followed by red fruit. Unique rose-pink mottled leaves mature to deep purple and in fall turn pink-purple. Height: 90–100cm; width: 60–90cm. Sun.

Caragana 'Weeping'
Caragana arborescens 'Pendula'

Graceful weeping branches highlight this feature plant. It looks terrific in shrub beds or rockeries. Covered in masses of yellow blooms in early summer. Heat and drought tolerant. Height: graft dependant; width: 2–3m. Sun.

Potentilla 'Goldfinger'
Potentilla fruticosa

Potentillas are extremely adaptable and easy to grow shrubs with good heat and drought tolerance. 'Goldfinger' presents large, bright yellow blooms all summer on a dense form. Height: 90–100cm; width: 90–100cm. Sun to P.M. sun.

Spruce 'Nest'
Pice abies 'Nidiformis'

This low-growing spruce usually has a slight depression on the top that makes it look like a nest. Its new growth contrasts with older dark green needles on a flat-topped, bun-shaped form—great in shrub beds and borders. Height: 1m; width: 1.5m in 15–20 years. Sun.

Spruce 'Nest'

Caragana 'Weeping'

Success in gardening beneath a tree is directly related to what you grow, and how much and how often you water.

I have a tall blue spruce in the corner of my back yard, and though I have removed the lower branches and raked up all of the fallen needles, nothing that I plant seems to grow around it. Friends tell me to put gravel underneath it and be done with it, but I'm not ready to give up yet. What grows here?

MOST PEOPLE ARE under the impression that it's the shade these trees cast and the acidity of their decomposing needles that limit what grows beneath them. Although it is true that, over time, both may be limiting factors, the amount of water these trees take up from the surrounding soil often makes it difficult to grow plants beneath the tree—they are, after all, competing for moisture, and in this case, a tall spruce will always win. One good solution is to mulch the soil beneath and around the tree with attractive pinecones and set containers filled with colourful annuals on top. (Remember that these trees will continue to shed needles and drop sap, so choose mulching material wisely.) Many perennials will grow in this situation, but you may not get a nice, even carpet of foliage. Success will be directly related to how much and how often you water.

ANNUALS

ANNUALS

Lobelia, Regatta Series

Masses of tiny flowers make trailing lobelia a favourite for use in hanging baskets and containers. Available in blue, lavender, pink and white shades. Height: 7–10cm; trails to 30cm. A.M. or P.M. sun.

FRUIT

Raspberry 'Arctic Groundcover'
Rubus arcticus

A great novelty groundcover offering blooms and fall foliage colour. Pink-purple flowers in early spring develop into small, fire-engine red fruits with wonderful flavour in summer. Light yields in the first year. Height: 8cm; spread: 30cm. Sun to A.M. sun.

PERENNIALS

Common St.John's Wort
Hypericum perforatum

This plant has a long medicinal history and its leaves can be used in salads. A good groundcover for sharply drained, moist, moderately fertile soil. Bright yellow flowers in summer are followed with red fall foliage. Spreading habit. Height: 60–90cm; width: 45–60+cm. Sun.

Heartleaf Bergenia
Bergenia cordifolia

This versatile perennial grows in a wide range of soil and moisture conditions. Glossy, evergreen foliage tints purple in winter and pale to dark pink flowers

Common St.John's Wort

Cranesbill 'Sue Crug'

Raspberry 'Arctic Groundcover'

Lobelia 'Regatta Mix'

bloom in spring. Do not cut back in fall. Clump-forming in habit. Height: 40–45cm; wide: 60cm. Sun or shade.

Cranesbill
Geranium 'Sue Crug'

Perennial geraniums are undemanding and long-lived plants that are clump-forming in habit. Striking magenta flowers with darker veins and center appear in late spring to fall. Height:

Ribbon Grass

50cm; width: 50–60cm. Prefers well-drained soil. Sun to P.M. sun.

Ribbon Grass
Phalaris arundinacea 'Feesey' (syn. 'Strawberries and Cream')

This pretty grass has a spreading habit. Its green and white striped foliage has a pink blush in cool weather. Spikelets turn to pinkish seed heads in summer. Prefers moist, well-drained soil but grows well in drier conditions. Height: 60–90cm; width: 60–90+cm. Sun or shade.

Russian Stonecrop
Sedum kamtschaticum

This sedum grows quickly and adapts to poor soils and dry periods making it a good groundcover. Yellow flowers appear in summer. Prefers well-drained, moderately fertile soil. Displays

Russian Stonecrop

Snow on the Mountain

succulent foliage and is clump-forming in habit. Height: 20–25cm; width; 30+cm wide. Sun to P.M. sun.

Snow on the Mountain
Aegopodium podagraria 'Variegatum'
An excellent groundcover, but it must be contained, otherwise it will spread into other plants and the lawn. It is useful planted in contained beds. It displays variegated foliage and creamy blooms in summer. Aggressive spreading habit—difficult to eradicate once established. Height: 30–60cm; width: 60+cm. Sun or shade.

Snow-in-Summer
Cerastium tomentosum
A great groundcover for poor soils and dry slopes, forming an attractive woolly, grey mat of foliage with white flowers appearing in late-spring to early summer. Too aggressive for the alpine rock garden but fine if monitored in a mixed bed. Cut back after blooming to keep compact and tidy. Prefers dry, well-drained soil. Height: 15–20cm; width: 90–100+cm. Sun.

Solomon's Seal
Polygonatum
This clump-forming plant has attractive, arching stems with pretty white flowers in spring—excellent for woodland gardens. Prefers moist, well-drained, organic soil. Clump-forming and upright in habit. Height: 45–60cm; width: 45–60cm. Shade to A.M. sun.

Solomon's Seal

Snow-in-Summer

The frame of a dead tree makes a striking garden sculpture and support for climbing vines, but be sure it is not a hazardous threat to people or property.

There is a dead tree in our backyard that has a striking, sculptural appearance. We want to leave it there and perhaps even spotlight it to enjoy its dramatic form at night. We're thinking of growing vines up it. What grows here?

It's fine to keep a dead tree in place as a sort of sculpture, as long as it's not also a hazardous tree: that is, one that could cause serious harm to pets, people or property should it fall down. (And it will fall, eventually.) Professional arborists should remove hazardous trees, and this service is worth every penny. If the tree can't cause any serious harm, then by all means dress it up with climbing roses or perennial or annual vines. The vines you choose may be self-supporting or may require netting or a trellis secured to the tree's trunk. You may also consider hanging baskets from limbs. Before you place plants at the tree's base, you'll want to deal with the underground components of the lighting you're considering installing.

ANNUALS

Black-Eyed Susan Vine, Sunny Series

This pretty annual vine displays curling tendrils, heart-shaped foliage and open-faced flowers in shades of lemon yellow and orange. Grow up a trellis or netting. Interesting used in hanging baskets. Height: 1.5–2m; spacing: 10–15cm. Sun.

Canary Bird Vine

This heat-loving, fast-growing annual vine requires support. It produces masses of tiny, yellow, 1cm, orchid-like flowers. Height: up to 4m; spacing: 25–30cm. Sun.

Morning Glory 'Heavenly Blue'

This vigorous annual, twining vine displays incredible, 10cm, pure sky-blue flowers that open early in the morning and are replaced by new blooms the next day. Requires support. Height: 2–3m; spacing: 30–45cm. Sun.

PERENNIALS

Golden Clematis
Clematis tangutica 'Golden Harvest'

Tanguticas are the largest, hardiest and most vigorous Clematis. They climb on support and also make great groundcovers for slopes or banks. Gold-yellow flowers appear in midsummer to fall followed by attractive seed heads. Prune back by a third in spring. Prefers well-drained soil. Heigth: 3–4m; width: 2–3m. Sun to P.M. sun.

Honeysuckle 'Dropmore Scarlet'
Lonicera x *brownii*

This perennial vine requires support and produces sweetly scented, orange-scarlet, tubular blooms in June to Sept. Do not cut back in fall. Height: 3–4m; width: 1–2m. Sun to P.M. sun.

ROSES

'John Cabot' Explorer
Hybrid Kordesii

This climbing rose is disease resistant and hardy to Zone 2. Double, medium red, 7–8cm flowers bloom repeatedly from early summer to frost. Light fragrance. Height: 3m; spread: 1.5–2m. Sun.

'John Cabot' Rose

Honeysuckle 'Dropmore Scarlet'

5
Tight Budgets
The Means to Garden

Time is money is the old saw we hear over and over again. Something that is often forgotten, though, is that if you don't have money, at least you still have time—at least when it comes to gardening.

Landscaping can be expensive or affordable— it just depends on what you spend and what you expect as a rate of return. Have you ever seen the instant front yard of a show home planted up with large shrubs and seemingly almost full-grown trees? These landscapes look pretty amazing, as if they've been established for quite awhile. Go back to that same neighbourhood in three, seven or ten years, and you'll note that the surrounding yards have pretty much caught up with the original show home and probably didn't cost quite as much to landscape.

When purchasing plants, keep this tip in mind: the bigger the plant, the greater the cost, for the simple reason that the greenhouse growers have spent more time, effort and space nurturing that plant. By the time it gets to the sales area, a significant investment has been made in that plant, so it's no mystery why it costs more than a packet of seed. A smaller specimen will likewise reflect a smaller investment on the grower's part—and it may be the better purchase for your circumstances.

I'm not saying you shouldn't purchase huge specimens. Rather, I'm saying don't be discouraged if you can't afford to. Remember plants grow and patience pays off. If you think about it, a tower poplar will grow to a mature height of, say, twenty metres, depending on where you live. Whether you buy a four-metre-tall tree for $100 or a one-metre-tall seedling for $10, they will both reach the same height in the end—you just have to be willing to wait an extra few years for the smaller tree to reach maturity.

When you don't have cash in hand, a little extra time becomes very valuable. You can save a tremendous amount of money simply by accepting a slower "rate of return." The difference between a budget-conscious garden and one constructed with unlimited funds can be summed up in one word: patience.

IN THE GARDEN

Christina and Pierre McDonald built an acreage home and were left with a limited landscaping budget.

They made the most of every dollar with careful research and planning. Time and money were first allocated to hardscaping and high-quality soil, followed by the bones of the garden, trees—all excellent investments for the long-term health and beauty of the yard. Then they turned to tasks that didn't cost much, if anything. They built a compost bin and created a holding bed where donated plants from friends and relatives, and "great deals" from the garden centre could be temporarily stored. Free tree chippings provided mulch that helped conserve water and keep weeds at bay.

After just four years, their garden is well established, and visitors believe it's much older. Christina and Pierre learned that when it comes to managing a tight gardening budget, patience and planning are priceless.

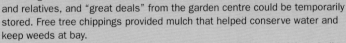

Selecting quick-growing perennials that can be divided in a few years is an economical way of increasing your plant stock.

We have a huge yard, a tiny budget and very little gardening experience! We are not sure where to start and want to try plants that will grow quickly and can be easily divided to plant throughout the garden. What grows here?

A NY GARDENER FACED with a large space and limited financial re- sources may feel overwhelmed by the task of creating a pleasing gar- den. Draw up a plan that can be implemented in stages, over a few years; this is far less costly and frustrating than trying to build a lush garden in a single season. Dividing plants is an excellent way to stretch garden- ing dollars and is not difficult—just remember to choose the appropriate dividing method for the type of plant you are working with. Large peren- nials are divided by using a sharp spade to split the plant in two. Small perennials can be divided by using a sharp knife to divide the root in two or three pieces. Make sure that each piece has a growing point and some roots. Some perennials can be easily pulled apart with your hands. Ensure that each set of leaves has its own stems and roots. Another way to expand your garden is to get to know other gardeners who are willing to share or trade their divided plants with you. This will help to increase the diversity in your yard at no expense.

PERENNIALS

Snowdrop Anemone
Anemone sylvestris

This pretty plant produces nodding, fragrant, pure white flowers in spring. These hardy plants benefit from dividing every three to five years. Prefers moist, organic, acidic, fertile soil. Height: 30–50cm; width: 45–60cm. Sun to P.M. sun.

Daylily
Hemerocallis 'Lady Scarlett'

Daylilies are hardy, versatile, clump-forming plants with grass-like foliage that are ideal for any mixed border. They benefit from dividing every three to five years. This variety blooms in July, offering true red flowers with a yellow-green throat and may re-bloom in fall. Height: 60–80cm; width: 45–75cm. Sun to P.M. sun.

Delphinium
Delphinium

Delphinium's upright habit benefits from a wind-sheltered location and may require staking. Divide every three to four years and cut back after flowering to promote re-blooming. This plant is a heavy feeder and benefits from regular fertilizing. Spiked, dark blue flowers with dark eyes bloom in summer. Prefers moist, fertile, well-drained soil. Height: 1–1.5m; width: 75–90cm. Sun to P.M. sun.

Greyleaf Cranesbill
Geranium cinereum 'Ballerina'

Perennial geraniums are undemanding, long-lived plants, suitable as a groundcover for a woodland or shrub bed. Clump-forming in habit and easily divided. 'Ballerina' has red-veined, lilac-pink flowers with red centers that bloom in late spring to summer and grey-green foliage. Prefers well-drained soil. Height: 10–15cm; width: 20–30cm. Sun to P.M. sun.

L.A. Hybrid Lily
Lilium 'Country Star'

A wonderful, hardy lily for the mixed border with interesting foliage and large, colourful flowerheads that make excellent cutflowers. Clump-forming in habit and easy to divide. The pale orange-yellow flowers that appear in early summer face upwards. Prefers fertile, well-drained, organic soil. Height: 1m; width: 30–45cm. Sun to P.M. sun.

Bearded Iris
Iris germanica 'Loganberry Squeeze'

Irises provide wonderful colour in the spring with spectacular flowers and their fans of foliage add interest to the garden throughout the growing season. Clump-forming and upright in habit, they are easily divided. Fragrant, raspberry-violet flowers bloom in early summer. Prefers moist, well-drained, fertile soil. Height: 90cm; width: 45–60cm. Sun.

Bearded Iris 'Loganberry Squeeze'

Delphinium

Collecting seed isn't difficult, but not all plants will produce offspring that look like their parents—a trait that can lead to a lively, ever-changing garden.

I'm on a very tight budget and simply cannot afford to buy annuals every year. I wondered about trying plants that I can grow from seed, collect the seed from or can be left to re-seed themselves. What grows here?

IT MAY APPEAR THAT GROWING all of your annuals from purchased and saved seed is a simple way of conserving your gardening dollars, and it can be, but you need to be aware of the costs for equipment (trays, grow lights, benches/tables and seedling soil mixes) and energy to run heating trays and grow lights. Choosing to grow plants that can be directly seeded outdoors will reduce or eliminate these costs. Remember when collecting seed from favourite plants (or allowing them to self-seed directly) that they may be hybrids and the seed may have enormous variability. You don't have to limit yourself strictly to annuals. Many perennials, trees and shrubs can be grown from seed, although it takes time for the latter two to grow into sizeable plants.

ANNUALS

Calendula 'Bon Bon Mix'

This easy-to-grow hybrid is a no-fuss annual that produces lovely double, daisy-like, 6–7cm flowers in cheery shades of apricot, orange and yellow. If not cut back it may self-seed, although not true to type, and seed is easily collected for distribution to other parts of the garden. Excellent in mass displays. Height: 30cm; spacing: 15–20cm. Sun to P.M. sun.

Four O'Clock 'Marvel of Peru Mix'

The seeds of Four O'clock are large and easy to handle, making them ideal for directly sowing outdoors. The fragrant flowers are a unique trumpet-shape and are available in red, white, yellow, pink and violet. Flowers open in the afternoon. Heat tolerant. Seed collected from plants will be true to type. Height: up to 60cm: spacing: 30–40cm. Sun.

Lavatera 'Silver Cup'

This annual favourite is easy to sow directly into the garden and any seed that is collected will be true to type. These bushy plants produce satiny, rose, cup-shaped flowers—very showy in the garden. Great in mass displays and is wind tolerant. Height: 60–90cm; spacing: 40–60cm. Sun.

Marigold, Gem Series

Your local garden centre will offer seeds of many varieties of marigolds that can be started indoors or seeded directly out into the yard. You can collect seed from this variety at the end of the season but they won't be reliably true to type. Colours available range from deep golden yellow, bronze, orange and cream. Very nice accent plants. Height: 30cm; spacing: 15–20cm. Sun.

Calendula 'Bon Bon Mix'

Four O'Clock 'Marvel of Peru Mix'

Lavatera 'Silver Cup'

Poppy 'Shirley Double'

Poppies are easy to gather seed from or to leave to self-seed. Excellent in mass displays, where their double, delicate flowers in shades of pink, red, salmon and scarlet can really make an impact. Height: 40–50cm; spacing: 20–30cm. Sun.

Sunflower 'Big Smile'

Sunflowers are perhaps the easiest annual to grow and, in the case of some varieties, to collect seed from, if the birds don't beat you to them! Many of the new varieties available do not go to seed, so choose carefully when purchasing packages. 'Big Smile' is a medium-sized variety that boasts black-centered, golden-yellow, 15cm flowers—excellent in borders. It produces seed that may not be true to type. Height: 30–40cm; spacing: 45–60cm. Sun.

Sweet Pea 'Explorer Mix'

The big round seeds of sweet peas are easy to handle and are sown directly into the garden. 'Explorer Mix' contains seven bright colours of fragrant, pretty flowers. The plants are fast-growing and bush-type, which means they do not require support. Height: 30–35cm; spacing: 25–30cm. Sun.

Sunflower 'Big Smile'

Poppy 'Shirley Double'

Sweet Pea 'Explorer Mix'

PERENNIALS

Alpine Poppy

Papaver nudicaule v. *croeceum*
(syn. P. croeceum) 'Flamenco'

This poppy, hailing from the slopes
Kazahkstan, is short-lived but self-sows
freely and naturalizes in a rock garden.
Orange to red flowers appear in summer above tufts of toothed foliage.
Prefers well-drained, poor soil. Height:
20–25cm; width: 20–25cm. Sun.

Black Violet

Viola 'Bowles' Black'

This violet self-sows very freely. It
displays attractive black-purple flowers
from spring to fall and is clump-forming in habit. Prefers well-drained, organic, moist, gritty soil. Height: 15cm;
width: 20–30cm. Sun to P.M. sun.

Perennial Blue Flax

Linum perenne

This clump-forming plant has fine
foliage and dainty, striking blue flowers
that last one day, produced over a long
period in summer. Self-seeds readily.
Prefers moist, well-drained soil but
adapts well to drier conditions. Height:
40–60cm; width: 30–45cm wide. Sun
to P.M. sun.

Perennial Blue Flax

Alpine Poppy 'Flamenco'

Black Violet 'Bowles' Black'

A colourful, well-kept landscape adds tremendous curb appeal and can help sell a home quickly.

My wife has just been transferred to another city and we need to sell our home quickly. The real estate agent suggested several things we could do to get top dollar for the house and has asked us to consider sprucing up the yard. We don't want to spend a lot of money and we need it to look good very quickly. What grows here?

A POTENTIAL BUYER must pass through the yard to get to your home. The landscape needn't be incredible, but it should look well kept and welcoming, and it's the simple things that make the biggest difference. Tidy the yard and put away tools and garbage receptacles. Take the time to edge, fertilize and mow the lawn. Remove dead or dying plants, and prune dead wood from trees and shrubs. Add curb appeal to the yard, and a little "wow" factor, by planting or purchasing some containers of colourful annuals. Place them in spots that highlight entrances and in areas that can been seen from windows. You can even set them in beds that require a shot of colour. Leave the containers as a house-warming gift for the new owners or take them to your new home to enjoy.

ANNUALS

Bacopa 'Abunda Giant White'

Bacopa has become a reliable favourite for containers, hanging baskets and mixed planters, providing nice contrast to larger annuals. It displays hundreds of white, single flowers on a low-growing form that spills and spreads over sides of pots. Heat tolerant. Height: 5–10cm; trails to 20cm. Sun.

Geranium, Designer Series

This series offers many rich colours with extra large, double flowers that make them an appealing accent plant—excellent in containers, flowerbeds and hanging baskets. Height: 30–35cm; spacing; 30–35cm. Sun to P.M. sun.

Marigold, Antigua Series

African marigolds are outstanding, undemanding plants that produce prolific double flowers. Antigua comes in shades of gold, orange, primrose and yellow and the plants have a compact, even growth habit—excellent in containers or borders. Weather tolerant. Height: 20–25cm; spacing: 20–25cm. Sun to P.M. sun.

Fall Mum 'Vicky Orange'

Annual mums come in a variety of beautiful colours and are stunning in containers. These plants help to add colour to the landscape well into fall and are quite frost tolerant. Height: 45cm spread: 45cm. Sun.

Pansy, Bingo Series

Pansies thrive in early spring and late fall due to their exceptional frost tolerance. Great in pots or planted out in the garden. The Bingo series displays large, 9cm flowers that show good heat tolerance. Height: 15cm; spacing: 15–20cm. Sun to P.M. sun.

Petunias, Madness Series

Petunias are such reliable plants for providing impact and colour from spring to early fall, whether in containers or planted out into the garden. The Madness series offers many shades of mixed, veined, 8cm, single flowers that are weather tolerant. Height: 25–30cm; spacing: 15–20cm. Sun to P.M. sun.

Fall Mum 'Vicky Orange'

Petunia, Madness Series

Geranium 'Designer Salmon Rose'

One economical way to enjoy gardening on a rental property is to grow a variety of plants in containers that can be taken with you when you move.

I am renting a home where I plan to live for a few years and am happy to take on the maintenance of the rather plain garden. Although I don't want to invest money in a property that I do not own, I do want a nice yard that I can entertain in and enjoy. I'd like to try growing a wide variety of plants. What grows here?

ONE OF OUR STAFF was in just such a situation and, being a plant enthusiast, he couldn't wait to have his own home to begin a plant collection. He gardened in containers filled with annuals, perennials and roses, and even planted a small vegetable and herb plot in an existing empty bed. Each fall he transfered perennials and roses he wished to save over winter to his sister's home, where he would plant them in her emptied vegetable garden. When he finally purchased his own home he enjoyed an advantage over other first-time homeowners in that he already had a cache of plants to start a garden. In your case, think about mobility and don't spend money on permanent plantings that can't be easily brought with you when the time comes to move on.

Begonia, Non-Stop Series

This series offers non-stop colour. with beautiful, large, double flowers displayed on plants with a mounding habit—excellent in hanging baskets, containers and flowerbeds. Begonia tubers can be over-wintered. Height: 20–25cm; spacing: 15–25cm. Shade to A.M. sun.

Pennisetum 'Fountain Grass'

This superb accent plant is very striking in containers. It produces ornamental grassy, arching foliage and rosy spiked seed heads. Heat and drought tolerant. Height: 60–90cm; spacing: 45–75cm. Sun to P.M. sun.

Rudbeckia 'Indian Summer'

A superb plant in mass displays, borders and containers. Produces loads of deep golden, semi-double, 15–25cm, daisy-like flowers with brown centres. Excellent cutflower. Height 50cm; spacing: 30cm. Sun.

Pennisetum 'Fountain Grass'

Rudbeckia 'Indian Summer'

Begonia 'Non-Stop Yellow'

PERENNIALS

Alumroot
Heuchera 'Amber Waves'

Heucheras are hardy plants that are prized for their attractive foliage and tiny blooms in summer. Ruffled, amber-gold foliage and tiny, light rose flowers on 30cm stalks highlight this variety—makes a great groundcover. May require replanting every two years in fall, as crowns tend to push upwards. Requires moist, fertile, well-drained soil. Height: 20cm; width: 45cm. Sun to P.M. sun.

Blanket Flower
Gaillardia 'Baby Cole'

A longer-lived, dwarf gaillardia that displays red and yellow flowers with maroon centers in summer, attracting butterflies. Prefers fertile, well-drained, dry soil but is tolerant of poor soil. Clump-forming in habit. Height: 15–20cm; wide: 15–20cm. Sun to P.M. sun.

Hosta
Hosta 'Gold Standard'

Hostas are very attractive grown in pots. This variety is fast-growing and is often used as a groundcover or as a specimen plant. Clump-forming in habit with light green-gold foliage edged in green. Prefers moist, fertile, well-drained, organic, slightly acidic soil. Height: 55cm; width: 1.5m. Shade to A.M. sun.

Alumroot 'Amber Waves'

Blanket Flower 'Baby Cole'

Hosta 'Gold Standard'

Mugwort
Artemisia vulgaris
'Oriental Limelight'
A tough, upright plant useful in difficult spots. A container is a great way to contain its aggressive habit and still enjoy its striking cream-and-green variegated foliage. Tolerates hot and dry sites and performs well in poor, well-drained, alkaline, dry soil. Height: 60–170cm; width: 30–100cm. Sun to P.M. sun.

Spike Speedwell
Veronica spicata
Often used in the front of a border combined with daylilies, tickseed or ornamental grasses. It is also quite pretty in a container. Blue, white or rose flowers appear in summer. Prefers organic, moist, well-drained soil. Height: 30–60cm; width: 45cm. Sun to P.M. sun.

Roses

'Barbra Streisand' Hybrid Tea
This is a lovely rose for a large patio pot. Stunning clustered, double blooms in lavender with a dark blush. The flowers open slowly releasing an intense rose-citrus fragrance. Blooms June through summer. Height: 1m; width: 1m. Sun.

Spring Bulbs

Dahlia 'Babylon Purple'
Dahlias make wonderful container plants and this variety of dinnerplate dahlia produces numerous, large, double, maroon flowers atop tall stems for a long season of display. Lift the tubers in fall and over-winter. Height: 1.5m; width: 1.5m. Sun.

'Barbra Streisand' Rose

Spike Speedwell

Dahlia 'Babylon Purple'

Snow on the Mountain is a very aggressive, very useful plant for controlling erosion and quickly covering bare soil, but you must contain its spread.

I need to cover a large area at the side of my home to stop soil erosion and keep weeds from taking over, but I don't have much cash to put into purchasing plants. What grows here?

PLANTS THAT ARE QUICK to cover an area are often deemed invasive and many gardeners shy away from growing them, out of fear they will take over their yards. This is where it pays to do a little research. When you're talking about eliminating soil erosion and forestalling weeds, it's critical that you choose the right plants. These plants must be quick to root, quick to spread and tough enough to thrive in the soil, light and temperature conditions of your particular problem spot. Choose plants that spread by runners or suckers, and contain them by installing underground barriers that prevent aggressive spreading. Avoid plants that set seed and will spread aggressively beyond the area you're concerned with. Don't be afraid to try unconventional solutions, such as vines grown horizontally along the ground.

ANNUALS

Petunia, Tidal Wave Series

A non-permanent, seasonal solution to erosion, 'Tidal Wave' can be grown as a spreading groundcover or tall hedge, depending how closely you space the plants. Available in many vibrant shades. Spacing 30cm apart results in plants growing up to 90cm tall. Spacing 60–75cm apart results in plants spreading up to 90cm. Sun to P.M. sun.

PERENNIALS

Cinquefoil

Potentilla neumanniana (syn. P. verna & tabernaemontai) 'Goldrush'

A creeping groundcover that may be invasive. Produces pretty yellow flowers in spring to summer. Prefers lean to moderately fertile soil and is drought tolerant. Height: 5–10cm; width: 30–45+cm. Sun.

Common Hops

Humulus lupulus

This vigorous climbing vine can be grown as a dense groundcover. Produces cone-like, green female flowers in summer. Usually cut back in fall but may be left to control erosion. Prefers well-drained, organic, moderately fertile soil. Height: 4–6m; width: 2–3+m. Sun to P.M. sun.

Snow on the Mountain

Aegopodium podagraria 'Variegatum'

An excellent groundcover, but it must be contained, otherwise it will spread into other plants and the lawn. It is useful planted in contained beds. It displays variegated foliage and creamy blooms in summer. Aggressive spreading habit—difficult to eradicate once established. Height: 30–60cm; width: 60+cm. Sun or shade.

TREES & SHRUBS

Juniper 'Effusa'

Juniperus communis

This juniper spreads to form a low, wide mat of attractive, dense evergreen foliage. New growth is light greenish-silver, aging to rich deep green. One the hardiest junipers and an excellent choice for a low maintenance situation. Height: 25–35cm; width: 2–3m. Sun.

Russian Cypress

Microbiota decussata

A great groundcover that spreads indefinitely in the right conditions. We know of a 14-year-old shrub that was four meters wide! Bright green foliage turns purple-brown in winter. Requires moist soil. Height: 30cm; width: 3–4m. Shade to A.M. sun.

Petunia, Tidal Wave Series

Juniper 'Effusa'

Cinquefoil 'Goldrush'

Plants make an excellent house-warming gift for the new homeowner—just be sure to pass on any helpful growing tips.

Our son and daughter-in-law have just moved into their first home. They don't have much money for landscaping (or much experience). They're thrilled that family and friends have offered to buy them plants for the yard as house-warming gifts. I have a very limited budget and want to be sure to buy them a tree or shrub that will survive. What grows here?

YOU ARE LOOKING FOR A PLANT that will really perform and, from the sounds of your son and daughter in-law's level of experience, one that won't be too fussy. Buying a tree or shrub for them isn't too far removed from buying them a pet—both require a degree of care and responsibility. There are a few steps you can take to achieve your goal: determine what hardiness zone they live in and do a little research at a local garden centre. There, with some knowledgeable assistance, you can see first-hand some of the most reliable plants available locally. Ask about times when stock is likely to go on sale and always inquire into the details of the centre's growing guarantee. Pass on any growing information that you can to the kids. The plants listed here make great gifts that are easy to grow with excellent results—sure to boost a novice gardener's confidence.

PERENNIALS

Asiatic Lily
Lilium 'Pink Pagoda'

Asiatic lilies are unmatched for wonderful blooms in the summer perennial bed. These clump-forming plants are pest-resistant and hardy, producing blooms that make excellent cutflowers. 'Pink Pagoda' displays soft pink flowers with a rose eye in early summer and prefers fertile, well-drained, organic soil. Height: 60cm; width: 30–45cm. Sun to P.M. sun.

Daylily
Hemerocallis 'Raspberry Pixie'

Daylilies are hardy, versatile, clump-forming plants. This is a short variety and an extended bloomer (flowers last longer than a single day). Divide every three to five years. Fragrant raspberry-red blooms appear in July. Prefers moist, fertile, well-drained soil. Height: 30cm; width: 30–60cm. Sun to P.M. sun.

Hosta
Hosta 'Francee'

This is an elegant, award-winning variety that makes a great groundcover. It has forest-green, heart-shaped foliage edged in white. Prefers moist, fertile, well-drained, organic, slightly acidic soil. Height: 55cm; width: 1m. Shade to A.M. sun.

Daylily 'Raspberry Pixie'

Hosta 'Francee'

Peony
Paeonia 'Auguste Dessert'

Peonies are great low-maintenance, clump-forming plants that are hardy, vigorous and pest- and disease-resistant. They are slow-growing but very long-lived perennials. This variety boasts semi-double, light pink flowers in spring. Prefers moist, acid-free, fertile, well-drained soil. Height: 75cm; width: 75–90cm. Sun to P.M. sun.

Roses

'Winnipeg Parks' Parkland
Hardy Shrub

An absolutely lovely rose with almost fluorescent colour and a low, compact form. Hardy to Zone 2. Double, medium red, fading to dark red-pink on petal undersides, 7–9cm flowers bloom June to frost with a light fragrance. Height: 30–60cm; width: 30–60cm. Sun.

Trees & Shrubs

Chokeberry 'Autumn Magic'
Aronia melonocarpa

A really nice shrub with fragrant, clustered white blooms in spring followed by clusters of purple fruit. Striking red and orange fall colours. Height: 1.5–2m; width: 1.5–2m. Sun.

Chokeberry 'Autumn Magic'

'Winnipeg Parks' Rose

Cranberry 'Wentworth'
Viburnum trilobum

An excellent choice for screening and large shrub beds. Blooms heavily in spring with pretty white clustered flowers followed by high yields of edible and ornamental red fruits that make good juice and jellies. Foliage turns a strong red colour in fall. Prefers moist soil. Height: 3–4m; width: 3–4m. Sun to P.M. sun.

Linden 'Harvest Gold'
Tilia mongolica

A really nice gift tree, this narrow, up-right variety is perfect for small yards. Beautiful bark starts to peel attractively when trunk is 5 centimetres in diameter. Fragrant white blooms appear in summer. Foliage is a nice green-gold. Height: 10–15m; width: 6–7m. Sun.

Ninebark 'Diabolo'
Physocarpus opulifolius

'Diabolo' is a versatile and useful shrub as a feature in large shrub beds or for use as an informal hedge. It offers super contrast with rich purple foliage on strong, upright branches. Really attractive pink clustered blooms appear in early summer followed by interesting pink seed heads. Sometimes found in standard tree form. Height: 2–3m; width: 2–3m. Sun to P.M. sun.

Potentilla 'Abbotswood'
Potentilla fruticosa

Potentillas are extremely adaptable and easy to grow shrubs with good heat and drought tolerance. 'Abbotswood' presents masses of bright white blooms all summer on a dense form. Use in the shrub bed or even as a hedge. Height: 90cm; width: 90–100cm. Sun to P.M. sun.

Cranberry 'Wentworth'

Linden 'Harvest Gold'

Ninebark 'Diabolo'

Get the most out of a short growing season by planting bulbs like 'Ice Follies' narcissus that naturalize and bloom reliably early each spring.

We have a short growing season where we live, and I'd like to extend it by planting bulbs that will bloom reliably in spring and maybe even multiply and spread. I don't have a lot of cash to spend. What grows here?

BULBS ARE A GREAT WAY to get the most out of a short growing season. In fact, not only can you plant bulbs that get spring off to a colourful start, but you can also grow bulbs, such as colchicum, that bloom into the fall season. Naturalized bulbs are those that remain in the ground all year and multiply, spreading throughout an area. Choose species bulbs, not the named, hybridized varieties (there are some exceptions however, such as specific narcissus hybrids). While most hybrid bulbs—for example, Rembrandt tulips—often provide a flashier show than species variet-ies, they won't last much more than a single season. Species bulbs, on the other hand, will self-propagate and gradually spread across the yard. Some bulbs, such as scillas, are quite inexpensive. Spread out the cost by adding a few new bulbs each year.

FALL BULBS

Crocus
Crocus chrysanthus 'Fuscotinctus'

This variety of early spring-blooming crocus produces sweet honey-scented, yellow flowers with purple stripes on the outer petals. Naturalizes readily in turf, rock gardens and borders. Prefers well-drained, slightly sandy, moderately fertile soil but adapts to most soils, provided they are well-drained. Height: 8–10cm; plant 10cm deep and 3–5cm apart. Sun to P.M. sun.

Iris
Iris reticulata 'Harmony'

Suitable for woodland, rock gardens and mixed beds. Produces light, sweetly scented, cornflower-blue flowers with a yellow ridge and white blotches in early spring. Hardy to Zone 3 with a protective mulch. Prefers a warm, sheltered location and sandy, well-drained, alkaline soil. Drier summer soils are required. Height: 5–10cm: plant 7–10cm deep and 6–10cm apart. Sun to P.M. sun.

Narcissus
Narcissus 'Ice Follies'

A large-cupped daffodil with white flowers with a canary-yellow cup. Blooms in early spring. Dry, not too hot soil is necessary for summer dormancy. Naturalizes well and is recommended for forcing indoors. Height: 30–50cm; 15–20cm deep and 8cm apart. Sun to P.M. sun.

Scilla
Scilla siberica

Each bulb produces three to four stems of nodding, bell-shaped, bright true-blue flowers in very early spring. Excellent choice for rock gardens, woodland gardens and mixed borders. It will not tolerate hot, dry conditions and prefers organic, well-drained, moist soil. Height: 5–10cm; plant 8cm deep and 4–5cm apart. A.M. or P.M. sun.

Tulip
Tulip kaufmanniana
'Heart's Delight'

The earliest flowering hybrid tulip. Produces more than one flower per stem. Naturalizes easily and is hardy and weather-resistant. Blooms in very early spring producing carmine-red flowers edged milky-pink, with pale pink interior and a yellow throat. Prefers organic, well-drained soil. Height: 10–20cm; plant 15–20cm deep and 3–9cm apart. Sun.

Tulip
Tulipa tarda

Very reliable, persisting for many years with little care. Multiplies readily by stolons. Produces fragrant, bright-yellow flowers with white tips. Each stem produces 5 or 6 flowers. Prefers well-drained, lean, gravelly soil. Height: 12–15cm; plant 12–20cm deep and 5–15cm apart. Sun to P.M. sun.

Tulip kaufmanniana 'Heart's Delight'

Iris 'Harmony'

Meadow gardens are loose, informal plantings that provide wave after wave of ever-changing colour.

My backyard consists of just a lawn of overgrown grass. I would like to make a meadow garden but I have no money for landscaping this year. What grows here?

THE BEAUTY OF MEADOW GARDENS is that they're open to all kinds of interpretation, since a meadow is simply an opening in a forest, encompassing any combination of plants from grass to daisies. If you don't have the funds to purchase plant or seeds this year, then one no-cost solution is to mow the grass in interesting paths or patterns throughout the yard, perhaps in a checkerboard or maze pattern. Over the winter purchase annual, biennial and perennial seeds and seed blends that catch your fancy, but be aware that many plants traditionally used in meadow gardens self-seed prolifically and will spread beyond your borders if not deadheaded. Next year you can begin stripping lawn and adding clean, weed seed-free compost and soil. Then simply sow your seeds directly out into the yard. One of the greatest challenges in a meadow garden is battling weeds, so be sure to start with a clean, weed-free site.

ANNUALS

Poppy 'Shirley Single'

Poppies are easy to gather seed from or to leave to self-seed. Excellent in mass displays, where the delicate, papery flowers in shades of pink, red, salmon and scarlet can really make an impact. Height: 40–50cm; spacing: 20–30cm. Sun.

PERENNIALS

Common Yarrow
Achillea millefolium

Yarrow is very heat and drought tolerant with flowers held in clusters atop foliage. Blooms early summer to late summer and has an upright habit. Tolerant of poor, dry soil. Height: 30–60cm; width: 40–60+cm. Sun to P.M. sun.

European Columbine
Aquilegia vulgaris 'Woodside'

This clump-forming plant with variegated foliage presents large flowers in late-spring in mixed colours. Prefers fertile, well-drained, moist soil. Height: 45–60cm; width: 30–45cm. Sun to P.M. sun.

Globe Centaurea
Centaurea macrocephala

A very large, dominant plant for the back of the border. Produces large, fuzzy, thistle-like, yellow flowers in late-spring to late summer on shiny brown bracts. Attracts bees. Drought tolerant but prefers moist, fertile, well-drained soil. Clump-forming in habit. Height: 90–100cm; width: 90–100cm. Sun to P.M. sun.

Iceland Poppy
Papaver nudicaule

Poppies are versatile plants that grow in many soil conditions. Self-seeds prolifically. Produces papery-thin flowers in spring to fall. Clump-forming in habit. Height: 30–45cm; width: 15–30cm. Sun to P.M. sun.

Maltese Cross
Lychnis chalcedonica

A splash of brilliant red colour held atop upright stiff stems—grow in a cottage garden or mixed border. Self-seeds and attracts hummingbirds. Cross-shaped, scarlet-red flowers bloom in early summer to midsummer. Prefers moist, fertile soil. Height: 90–120cm; width: 20–30cm. Sun to P.M. sun.

Common Yarrow

European Columbine 'Woodside'

6
Wind &
Weather

Facing Reality

Weather is a powerful force that affects what we are able to grow in any location. But it also has an effect on what we *believe* we can grow—and we are often mistaken.

We tend to let hardiness zone ratings become the primary tool that explains our climate, and we mistakenly let it dictate what we grow. In fact, zone ratings are only meant to be a guide, not an absolute indicator.

The information used to give a zone rating to a region is based on many factors—factors that don't consider the particular conditions of your yard. These microclimates are either cooler or warmer than your overall zone. For example, there are spots close to buildings or fences that absorb and radiate heat, enough heat to make a tender plant reliably perennial. Conversely, there are also depressions in the ground where cold air pools—a bad place to plant a tomato, even if you live in Zone 7.

People take zone ratings pretty seriously. I've seen gardeners get really upset because we sell plants rated Zone 4 in our Zone 3 greenhouse. On the surface, growing only plants that are rated to your zone seems like the best way to avoid losing plants, but the fact remains that the zone ratings on plant labels are often, at best, educated guesses. I've seen dozens of varieties rated as Zone 4, 5 or even 6 growing just fine in my Zone 3 location. Sure, some plants have gone through trials in many different zones and microclimates, but many more plants have not been thoroughly tested. A small amount of anecdotal evidence may be all that determines the zone rating. We don't use zone ratings in most of our books (or at our greenhouse) precisely because of these problems.

Of course I'm not suggesting that Zone 10 plants can be grown without fear in Zone 1. Check the zone rating, by all means—but then check with your friends and the local nursery staff to see how far you can push the zone boundaries. The key is to understand and accept the seasonal patterns of your location, learn to work with them and then experiment. If you learn to do that, then you'll really be in the zone.

IN THE GARDEN

Stephen Raven loves hybrid tea roses, but he lives in a Zone 3 region.

He has many years of experience with the incredibly variable weather of northern Alberta, and he knows what he must do to make tender roses survive.

Stephen starts off by choosing the hardiest varieties available and considering carefully where they might best survive in his yard. Some of his favourites need special care to make it through the winter: they must be cut back, mulched, placed in rose huts, and carefully watered and fertilized. If a variety doesn't work out, he gets rid of it or, if he really loves it, tries another location in the yard, hoping to take advantage of microclimates.

Wind and weather may sometimes frustrate gardeners, but there's nothing more satisfying to Stephen than successfully nurturing a plant through challenging winter conditions and reaping the rewards of blooms and fragrance the following spring.

Road salt spray can be really tough on plants, but there are a few, such as 'Creeping Blue' spruce, that are tolerant of moderate amounts of it.

The lovely border that I so carefully planned and planted along the curbside of my front yard is suffering terribly. The evergreens have browned and my shrubs are not leafing out well. I blame the road salt that is constantly applied to the road in winter for the dismal state of these plants. What grows here?

ROAD SALT IS OCCASIONALLY a necessary evil. Is it better to leave the streets unsalted and risk accidents (some of which could even destroy plants), or should we keep salting the streets and risk poisoning our curbside plants? As long as Canadian winters exist, we're going to take measures to keep cars from skidding all over the place, and for now, salt is the cure. The application of road salt to city streets can lead to serious problems for some plants. The airborne salt spray launched by vehicle tires coats plants and inhibits their normal growth. Cultivate plants that have natural tolerance to road salt, pile snow around roadside plantings or at the very least, construct a fence of burlap on the street side of the border to offer some protection to sensitive plants.

PERENNIALS

Sea Thrift
Armeria maritima 'Alba'

This clump-forming plant displays grass-like evergreen foliage. Tolerant of poor soils—perfect for rock gardens or front borders. Blooms in summer with ball-like, white flowers. Deadhead regularly to prolong blooming. Prefers well-drained soil. Height: 10–15cm; width: 30cm. Sun to P.M. sun.

ROSES

'Dwarf Pavement' Pavement
Shrub

Pavement roses are tough rugosa hybrids that have a low, sprawling habit. They may be the most salt-tolerant rose and are named to reflect their suitability for use as street-side plants. 'Dwarf Pavement' offers mildly fragrant, semi-double, dark pink, 6–8cm flowers that repeat through summer. Height: 75–90cm; width: 90cm. Sun.

TREES & SHRUBS

Burning Bush 'Turkestan'
Euonymus nanus var. *turkestanicus*

An excellent feature or accent shrub for foundation plantings. Plant in groups or singly. Foliage turns a flaming red colour in fall and the bleeding heart-like, pink and orange blooms appear in summer. Prefers moist, well-drained soil. Height: 1–1.5m; width: 1.5–2m. Sun or shade.

Russian Olive
Elaegnus angustifolia

A round-headed, small tree that is also sold in shrub form. Silvery leaves and dark bark contrast well with evergreen backgrounds. Very fragrant, tiny, yellow blooms appear in June. Thrives in a hot, dry site. Height: 6–10m; width: 6–10m. Sun.

Sea Buckthorn
Hippophae rhamnoides

The female plant has masses of bright orange berries in the fall, lasting all winter. Can be grown as a small tree or shrub. Displays dense, willow-like, silvery-grey foliage. Height: 3–6m; width: 3–6m. Sun.

Spruce 'Creeping Blue'
Picea pungens 'Glauca Procumbens'

This very attractive evergreen can be trained to to climb over rocks and small walls. Features bright silvery-blue needles that form a dense, slow-growing mat—excellent for large rock gardens. Height: 30–60cm; width: 4–6 m. Sun.

Sea Thrift 'Alba'

Russian Olive

'Dwarf Pavement' Rose

Not sure what grows well in your area? The staff at a reputable local garden centre can be a valuable resource for current information.

We have recently moved to an area that is classified as hardiness Zone 2. I'm not sure what to plant that will bloom or produce fruit or vegetables in such a short growing season. What grows here?

ONE OF THE BEST WAYS to figure out what grows in your new zone is to take note of what the neighbours are growing. Join a gardening club, visit local greenhouses and talk with those in the know about what they are growing. There are several strategies you can apply to get a jump on the spring and extend the growing season through the early fall: buy vegetable and bedding plants already started from a nursery, start your own seeds indoors, and use cold frames and greenhouses. Also consider buying shrubs that bloom on old or established wood, and avoid plants that bloom in the late fall in other zones (they won't produce much for you in the way of blooms). That being said, don't be afraid to experiment. There is no such thing as a "pure" climate zone, no matter where the garden is. Trees, foundations, slopes, hills, depressions—all can create microclimates that are either warmer or colder than the prevailing zone. The zone designation should be a starting point, not a hard and fast rule.

ANNUALS

Pansy, Imperial Series

Pansies thrive in early spring and late fall due to their exceptional frost tolerance—great in pots or planted out in the garden. Large 8cm flowers are available in soft pastel apricot, cream, orange and salmon. Height: 15–20cm; spacing: 15–20cm. Sun to P.M. sun.

FRUIT

Raspberry 'Red River'
Rubus

This raspberry produces fruit on new wood and has heavy yields of red, sweet and tangy berries that are great for processing. Cut back to 30cm each fall, in late August. Height: 90–100cm; spreads: 90cm. Sun.

PERENNIALS

Alpine Aster
Aster alpinus

Pink, blue or white flowers appear in spring—a reliable bloomer for rock gardens. Prefers well-drained, fertile soil. Clump-forming and spreading in habit. Height: 10–20cm; width: 30cm. Sun.

Golden Clematis
Clematis tangutica

Tanguticas are the largest, hardiest and most vigorous clematis. They climb on supports and also make great groundcovers for slopes or banks. Bright yellow, nodding bell flowers appear in late spring to fall followed by attractive seed heads. Prune back by a third in spring. Prefers well-drained soil. Height: 4–5m; width: 2–3m. Sun to P.M. sun.

ROSES

'David Thompson' Explorer
Hybrid Rugosa

The least thorny of the Explorer rose series. Although classed as medium-red, the colour is closer to deep fuschia.

Double, medium red, 7–8cm flowers with a light fragrance bloom profusely July to frost. Height: 1m; width: 1m. Sun.

VEGETABLES

Tomato 'Bush Early Girl'

The little sister to 'Early Girl,' this medium-sized tomato produces high yields of 200g fruit on compact, bush-like plants—terrific flavour. Matures in mid July. Use a cage and do not prune. Sun.

Alpine Aster

Pansy, Imperial Series

Don Heimbrecher of Calgary, Alberta grows a wide variety of hardy and tender roses very successfully in an area noted for its challenging climate.

I've recently taken up gardening and am very keen on establishing a rose bed. I live in quite a cold area and I'm not sure that the beautiful roses I see in gardening magazines will over-winter in our climate. What grows here?

THE ROSES YOU'RE ENAMOURED WITH are probably hybrid tea roses, and they can over-winter in fairly cold zones, provided they have lots of protection from winter weather (and a little luck). Most people don't want to go to all the extra trouble of protecting hybrid teas, so the ideal solution is to choose hardy roses. There are numerous hardy roses that bloom reliably in Zone 3, and even Zone 1, with no winter protection at all, save snow cover. Two series in particular, Explorer and Parkland (both developed in Canada), are very tough and provide a nice range of flower colours and plant heights. Rugosa roses are also extremely hardy, producing attractive crinkled foliage and fragrant blooms. If you are keen on growing tender roses and want the best over-wintering odds, plant some of the English roses. They often survive better in cold areas with a thick layer of protective mulch than do hybrid tea roses.

ROSES

'Alexander Mackenzie' Explorer
Shrub

This lovely rose produces a profusion of cup-shaped flowers in clusters of six to twelve and is hardy to Zone 1. Single, medium red, 6–7cm flowers appear from July to frost. Grow as a climbing rose. Height: 2m; width: 2m. Sun.

'Foxi Pavement' Pavement
Hybrid Rugosa

Pavement roses have a low, sprawling habit. They may be the most salt-tolerant roses and are named to reflect their suitability as street-side plants. 'Foxi' produces single, deep pink, 6–8cm flowers repeatedly all summer followed by deep red rosehips. Strong fragrance. Height: 75–90cm; width: 100cm. Sun.

'Furstin von Pless' Shrub
Hybrid Rugosa

This bushy, upright shrub is disease-resistant and sports crinkly, medium green foliage and double, clear white, 8–9cm flowers in early summer. Strong fragrance. Height: 1m; width: 1m. Sun.

'Jens Munk' Explorer
Hybrid Rugosa

This rose is hardy to Zone 1. Double, medium pink marked with a striking white streak, 6–7cm flowers bloom abundantly all summer. Spicy fragrance. Height: 1.5m; width: 2m. Sun.

'Morden Sunrise' Parkland
Hardy Shrub

Striking and unusual blooms are set off against glossy foliage on a small bushy rose. Semi-double, yellow with orange and pink overtones, 8–9cm flowers with a light fragrance bloom June through summer. Height: 60–75cm; width: 60–75cm. Sun.

'Red Frau Dagmar Hartopp' Shrub
Hybrid Rugosa

A hardy, tough rose with characteristically crinkled, medium green foliage. Single to semi-double, silvery red, 8–9cm flowers with a light fragrance bloom in early summer, repeating. Height: 1–1.5m; width: 1–1.5m. Sun.

'Red Frau Dagmar Hartopp' Rose

'Furstin von Pless' Rose

'Alexander Mackenzie' Rose

'Foxi Pavement' Rose

A number of plants, such as Sweet Joe Pye, can bloom right through cool fall weather until the first hard frost.

I have carefully planned my gardens to provide colour all spring and summer. Last year I attempted to use perennial asters to extend flowering into the fall. They grew very well but didn't bloom before the heavy frost hit. What grows here?

MOST LIKELY THE VARIETY of aster that you planted is one that blooms later rather than earlier in fall, and the reason is over your head—literally! The sun dictates when asters bloom. They are obligate short-day plants, meaning that they must have several weeks of short days to trigger flowering. Even though the variety you planted grew well, it probably didn't have enough consecutive short days followed by a long enough spell of warm weather. They simply ran out of time to bloom before the cold weather arrived. Try to select plants that reliably bloom three to four weeks before the first frost date for your region. As for perennial asters, try *Aster novae-angliae*, one of the earliest to bloom, followed by *Aster* x *dumosus* and finally *Aster novi-belgii*.

ANNUALS

Aster 'Serenade Mix'

A lovely annual aster that blooms from midsummer through fall. The flowers make great cutflowers, lasting up to three weeks in a vase. Serenade offers 3cm, semi-double blooms in shades of blue, carmine, light blue, red, rose, scarlet and bicolours. Height: 60cm; spacing: 20–30cm. Sun to P.M. sun.

Flowering Cabbage 'Dynasty Mix'

An excellent frost-resistant accent plant with a compact habit featuring white, pink and red, semi-waved foliage. Prefers a cool location. Height: 15–30cm; spacing: 30cm. Sun.

Rudbeckia 'Autumn Colours'

Annual rudbeckias display their large, bold flowers atop stiff stems. They make excellent, long-lasting cutflowers and hold up to mild frost. This variety has golden, 12cm, daisy-like flowers sporting brown centres with vivid red rings—great in containers or flowerbeds. Height: 50cm; spacing: 30cm. Sun.

Aster 'Serenade Mix'

Flowering Cabbage 'Dynasty Mix'

Rudbeckia 'Autumn Colours'

ANNUALS

Pansy, Bingo Series

Pansies thrive in early spring and late
fall due to exceptional frost tolerance.
The Bingo series produces fragrant,
large, 9cm flowers that face straight up.
Available in many beautiful colours.
Height: 15cm; spacing: 45–60cm. Sun.

PERENNIALS

Black-Eyed Susan
Rudbeckia hirta

Blooms from summer to first frost,
displaying golden-yellow flowers with
dark brown centres. Use to brighten up
a mixed border or as a cutflower. Tolerates poor, dry soils but does best in
well-drained, fertile, moist soil. Clump-
forming in habit. Height: 60–90cm;
width: 30–45cm. Sun to P.M. sun.

New England Aster
Aster novae-angliae
'Harrington's Pink'

This variety is suitable for any mixed
border and produces salmon-pink flowers in late summer to fall. Water at the
plant's base and avoid overcrowding.
Clump-forming in habit. Prefers well-
drained, fertile soil. Height: 75–100cm;
width: 50–75 cm. Sun to P.M. sun.

Purple Coneflower
Echinacea purpurea

Coneflowers are wonderful perennials for any mixed border. They attract butterflies and make an excellent
cutflower. Reflexed, purple flowers
with attractive centers bloom in summer to fall. Clump-forming in habit.
Prefers well-drained soil. Height: 90–
150cm; width: 45cm. Sun to P.M. sun.

Pansy 'Bingo Blue Frost'

Black-Eyed Susan

New England Aster 'Harrington's Pink'

Purple Coneflower

Solitary Clematis
Clematis integrifolia

Native to Europe, Russia and Asia, this attractive species is valuable for the mixed border. Nodding, twisted, bell-shaped, dark blue flowers appear in summer to fall. Prefers well-drained, fertile soil and cool roots. Bushy habit. Height: 90–100cm; width: 60–90cm. Sun to P.M. sun.

Sweet Joe Pye
Eupatorium purpureum

One of the showiest perennials! It forms a large, clump-forming, upright bush that contrasts well with evergreens and attracts butterflies. Fragrant, clustered, rose-purple flowers bloom late in summer to fall. Prefers moist, alkaline soil. Height: 90–150cm; width: 90–100cm. Sun to P.M. sun.

TREES & SHRUBS

Hydrangea 'Endless Summer'
Hydrangea macrophylla

This hydrangea is very hardy, producing blooms in summer that can remain on the plant well into fall. Flower colour will be pink in alkaline soil and blue in acidic soil. Dark glossy green foliage displays 18–20cm, pink or blue, globe-shaped clustered blooms. Height: 75–90cm; width: 75–90cm. A.M. to P.M. sun.

Sweet Joe Pye

Hydrangea 'Endless Summer'

Solitary Clematis

Keep your landscape interesting throughout the year by growing a variety of evergreens and deciduous trees and shrubs with striking form and foliage.

My garden is just lovely from late spring to late summer. I'm finding it less interesting in the early spring, fall and winter months. I've heard people talk about providing all-year interest. What grows here?

LOTS OF PEOPLE ARE SATISFIED with a garden that provides them with flowers during the summer. That's perfectly all right, but they are missing out on plants that give structure, form and contrast to their gardens—in spring and summer and beyond to the cooler periods of the year. It's easy to get into the mindset that gardening has a beginning and an end, when it's really a continuum. In the show garden at our greenhouse, we often see gentians blooming in November, rockcress blooming in March, calamagrostis grasses waving in the winter winds, and golden and red-twigged dogwoods creating an incredible contrast to the white snows of January. It takes a shift in thinking to achieve a year-round garden, but once you've accomplished that shift, you'll never go back to summer-only gardening.

PERENNIALS

Blue Oat Grass
Helictotrichon sempervirens

Grasses offer texture, variety of form and a sense of movement in the garden. This grass provides excellent contrast with other perennials or shrubs, particularly those with purple, yellow or silver foliage. Clump-forming in habit with blue, spiky foliage and arching, tan seed heads in summer. Prefers fertile, well-drained, alkaline soil. Height: 90–100cm; width: 60cm. Sun to P.M. sun.

Alpine Clematis
Clematis alpina 'Pink Flamingo'

Produces a lush, pest-free screen early in spring. Grow as a very hardy climber with support, groundcover or trailing over stone walls. Pretty semi-double, nodding, pink blooms in spring. Requires fertile, well-drained soil and cool roots. Do not cut back. Height: 2–3m; width: 2m. Sun.

Whitlow Grass
Draba rigida

This cushion-forming plant has evergreen foliage covered in bright yellow flowers in early spring and may re-bloom in fall. An excellent addition to a rock garden or alpine bed. Requires gritty, fertile, sharply drained soil. Do not cut back—avoid excessive water on foliage. Height: 5–10cm; width: 10–20cm. Sun to p.m. sun.

Alpine Clematis 'Pink Flamingo'

Blue Oat Grass

Whitlow Grass

Prairie Crocus

Pulsatilla patens
(syn. *Anemone patens)*

Native Prairie Crocus is clump-forming in habit with fern-like foliage and
lovely blooms that become fluffy seed
heads. Mauve-pink flowers, sometimes
cream, appear in early spring. It resents
being moved. Prefers moist, sharply
drained, fertile soil. Height: 10–15cm;
width: 10–20cm. Sun to P.M. sun.

Stemless Gentian

*Gentiana acaulis (*syn. *G. kochiana)*

These plants are prized for their flowers
in shades of true blue—a difficult colour to find. Large, blue flowers appear
in spring to summer. Requires organic, moist, well-drained soil. Height:
10–15cm; width: 20–30cm. Shade to
A.M. sun.

Prairie Crocus

Stemless Gentian

TREES & SHRUBS

Birch 'Young's Weeping'

Betula pendula 'Youngii'

A strongly weeping tree that needs
training to achieve a specific height,
at which point it will weep down and
may even cover the ground. This species is often grafted on a 1.5–2.5m
single stem—a beautiful feature tree for
small yards. Produces catkins in spring.
Bright white bark is attractive in all
seasons and the branches are lovely
covered in frost. Height: training dependant. Sun.

Dogwood 'Red Osier'

Cornus stolonifera

Dogwoods consistently offer attractive
bark that makes their form very showy
in winter. This large shrub has dark-
green leaves on bright-red branches
and white berries. An excellent choice
for mass plantings. Height: 3m; width:
3m. Sun to P.M. sun.

Juniper 'Tolleson's Weeping'

Harry Lauder's Walkingstick
Corylus avellana 'Contorta'

An interesting feature shrub that is trainable to a small tree. Displays showy spring catkins and unique curled branches and leaves. Remove any shoots originating below ground as these take over the plant and destroy its unique growth habit. Plant in a wind-protected site. Height: 1.5–3m; width: 1.5–3m. Sun to P.M. sun.

Juniper 'Tolleson's Weeping'
Juniperus scopulorum

A striking feature plant, ageing to its best form. Silver-blue foliage hangs mane-like from long arching branches—very attractive in all seasons. Height: 5–7m; width: 2–3 m. Sun.

Maple 'Amur'
Acer tataricum ssp. *ginnala*

A beautiful feature for small yards that can be trained to a large bonsai-like form. This small, wide-spreading tree has fragrant blooms in spring and incredible orange-red fall colour with red, winged seeds. Height: 4–6m; width: 5m. Sun to P.M. sun.

Mountain Ash 'Oak-leaf'
Sorbus hybrida

A very nice feature tree for small yards. Displays oak-shaped leaves on an upright, oval-headed form. White clustered blooms appear in spring followed by large, true red fruit, which may last the winter. Very attractive orange-red fall colour. Requires well-drained soil. Height: 7–10m; width: 5–7m. Sun.

Dogwood 'Red Osier'

Birch 'Young's Weeping'

Mountain Ash 'Oak-leaf'

Maple 'Amur'

A combination of warm days and cool nights help develop this maple's beautiful fall colour.

I just love the gorgeous fall colours that I've seen in images of the eastern provinces. I want to duplicate these in my own prairie yard. What grows here?

THESE COLOURS ARE often associated with the mixed forests of provinces such as Quebec and Ontario. The prairies are noted for gorgeous, sunny fall days with crystal-clear blue skies, and a drive through the countryside reveals an awful lot of fall colour, albeit not as many of the intense reds and auburns prevalent in eastern Canada. Fall brings shorter days and cooler temperatures that trigger chlorophyll (the pigment that gives leaves their green colour) to break down, revealing red, orange and yellow pigments. The process takes longer on some trees. In years when there is an early heavy frost, leaves may die before the colours fully develop. The intensity of foliage colour is controlled by weather. Warm, sunny fall days and cool fall nights (below 7°C) give the best colour. The eastern provinces generally have a longer autumn season that provides these conditions, as well as the climate to support some very colourful species. Other conditions affect colour too. The healthier your tree is, the better its fall show is likely to be. Good soil fertility and adequate moisture are also needed for nice autumn colour. You'll find that many trees, shrubs, perennials and annuals can put on a spectacular fall show in your area if the weather cooperates.

PERENNIALS

Himalayan Fleece Flower
Persicaria affinis 'Darjeeling Red'

A long-blooming evergreen ground-cover that produces spikes of pink flowers ageing to burnt red and foliage that turns red in fall. Flowers from early midsummer to fall. Great for front borders. Grows in a moist or dry area but prefers moist, fertile soil to produce a denser mat of foliage. Height: 15–25cm; spacing: 60–90+cm. Sun to P.M. sun.

Red Barrenwort
Epimedium x *rubrum*

Makes a delightful groundcover for difficult areas. Displays ruby-red flowers in spring and young foliage that is tinted red. The foliage reddens again in fall. Prefers organic, well-drained, moist soil but grows well in drier conditions. Clump-forming in habit. Height: 25–40cm; width: 30–45cm. Shade to A.M. sun.

TREES & SHRUBS

Cotoneaster 'Hedge'
Cotoneaster acutifolius

Also known as 'Peking'. A very hardy and useful shrub, traditionally sheared and shaped for formal hedging but equally as attractive left to arch in its natural form. Plant 30–45cm apart for hedges. Dark green, dense foliage turns a lovely orange-red colour in fall. Height: 2–3m; width: 2–3m. Sun to P.M. sun.

Red Barrenwort

Himalayan Fleece Flower 'Darjeeling Red'

Cotoneaster 'Hedge'

Cranberry 'Alfredo Compact'
Viburnum trilobum

An ideal, easy-to-grow shrub for hedging or borders. This extremely compact plant has very dense foliage turning a striking red fall colour. Produces bright red, edible fruits. Height: 1.5–2m; width: 1.5–2m. Sun to P.M. sun.

Dogwood 'Golden Prairie Fire'
Cornus alba

A great contrast or feature shrub that is very showy all year-round. It offers yellow foliage, fiery red fall colour and orange-red stems in winter. New stem growth is yellow. Height: 2–3m; width: 1.5–3m. Sun to P.M. sun.

Maple 'Tatarian'
Acer tataricum

This is a beautiful small tree for use in small yards that produces red-winged seeds in August and deep red and orange colour in fall. Blooms in May prior to leafing out. Height: 5–6m; width: 5–6m. Sun to P.M. sun.

Oak 'Northern Pin'
Quercus ellipsoidalis

'Northern Pin' is a bit faster growing than other oaks. It displays glossy summer foliage followed by striking russet-red foliage in fall. A hardy selection for northern areas. Height: 15–20m; width: 10m. Sun.

Ohio Buckeye

Serviceberry 'Autumn Brilliance'

Oak 'Northern Pin'

Ohio Buckeye
Aesculus glabra

This large, round-headed tree provides heavy shade and is best suited to large yards. Clustered creamy blooms in late spring are followed by interesting nuts covered with large spines. Produces super fall colour. Height: 10–15m; width: 10–15m. Sun to P.M. sun.

Serviceberry 'Autumn Brilliance'
Amelanchier x *grandiflora*

Serviceberry displays pretty pinkish-white blooms in spring and incredible red fall colour. This tree makes a very nice feature in a small yard. Avoid windy sites. Height: 6–7m; width: 4–6m. Sun to P.M. sun.

Sumac 'Laceleaf Staghorn'
Rhus typhina 'Laciniata'

Tropical-looking, finely dissected leaves make this an interesting plant in the border or used as screening. Greenish-yellow blooms appear in July. Produces striking red fall colour. Requires moist soil. Height: 2–3m; width: 4–5m. Sun to A.M. sun.

Cranberry 'Alfredo Compact'

Maple 'Tatarian'

Longleaf Lungwort 'Bertram Anderson' thrives in a shady bed and withstands wind well.

We have what essentially amounts to a shady, dry wind tunnel between our home and our neighbour's. Both ends of this space receive good sunlight, but it becomes progressively shadier towards the centre. We would like to incorporate plants into this area to reduce the strong winds and to make the area a little more attractive. What grows here?

YIKES! SHADY, DRY, WINDY—toss in bad soil and you've got the Four Horsemen of the Garden Apocalypse! To make matters worse, some city lots have as little as 2–2.5 metres of space between them, further limiting your options. You can't expect a garden of Eden in this sort of environment, but there are some tricks you can try. Inquire about sharing the space with your neighbour and erect a lattice-paneled trellis, set at an angle from the homes, with a narrow bed of shade-tolerant plants grown at its base. Planting a dense, columnar, medium-sized shrub or small tree at either or both of the sunny ends will also slow the wind, but may increase the shade toward the centre.

PERENNIALS

Alpine Clematis

Clematis alpina 'Pamela Jackman'

Grow as a very hardy climber with support, groundcover or trailing over stone walls. Produces nodding, blue flowers in spring and may re-bloom late in the season. Requires fertile, well-drained soil and cool roots. Do not cut back. Height: 3m; width: 2m. Sun to P.M. sun.

Big Petal Clematis

Clematis macropetala 'Markham's Pink' *(C. macropetala* v. *markhami)*

Double, open-face, pink flowers bloom in spring and are followed by attractive seed heads. The flowers produce the best colour in full sun. Requires fertile, well-drained soil and cool roots. Do not cut back. Height: 3–5m; width: 1–2m. Sun to P.M. sun.

Longleaf Lungwort

Pulmonaria longifolia 'Bertram Anderson'

A tough, clump-forming plant that is well suited as a groundcover for woodland or border edging. Displays silver-spotted foliage and deep violet-blue flowers in spring. Prefers fertile, well-drained, organic soil but is tolerant of poor soil. Height: 20–30cm; width: 45–60cm. Shade to A.M. sun.

Ostrich Fern

Matteuccia struthiopteris

This is a very popular, native, colony-forming fern with beautiful, arching fronds that resemble ostrich plumes. Requires moist, organic, well-drained, acidic soil. Height: 100–150cm; width: 60–75cm. Shade to A.M. sun.

TREES & SHRUBS

Juniper 'Blue Arrow'

Juniperus scopulorum

This variety of juniper is extremely narrow and upright in habit, useful for framing entrances. Displays intense deep blue foliage on a compact form that requires little or no shearing to maintain shape. Height: 5m; width: 60–90cm. Sun.

Ornamental Crabapple 'Dream Weaver'

Malus x *pumila*

A unique columnar form that has many uses in the landscape. Perfect for highlighting entrances, driveways and sunny sideyards. Deep burgundy-purple foliage highlights abundant pink blooms in spring. Height: 3m in 5–6 years; width: 30–60cm. Sun.

Ostrich Fern

Ornamental Crabapple 'Dream Weaver'

Sheltering your home and yard with a windbreak of shrubs and trees can cut heating and cooling costs substantially while creating micro-climates within the protected area.

We have a large lot that is located at the top of a hill. As a result, the conditions are very windy. We'd like to shelter the house and yard but we don't know what will stand up to the wind. What grows here?

WHEN I WAS GROWING UP on the farm, we planted miles of shelterbelt trees to protect our crops from cold, dry winds that tore across the fields. The microclimates created by those trees were phenomenal, and many years later they still make the difference between a great crop and no crop at all—particularly when it comes to heat-loving crops like corn and cucumbers. The shelterbelt also protected the house and its landscaping from cold winds and wind damage. Windbreaks are often planted three rows deep and include both deciduous and evergreen trees. The trade-off for the protection they offer is the moisture they extract from the soil and the shade they cast. Most city lots are not large enough to duplicate traditional farm windbreaks. Instead most people compromise by installing tall, semi-open fences bordered by high, narrow trees. A three-metre high windbreak can effectively give you protection up to 50 metres downwind.

Aspen 'Swedish Columnar'
Populus tremula 'Erecta'

Beautiful planted in groups as a screen or windbreak—good for small yards or tight spaces. This tree has shallow, non-invasive roots. Small round leaves tremble at the slightest breeze on a tall, columnar, hardy form. Height: 10m; width: 1.5–2m. Sun.

Caragana 'Sutherland'
Caragana arborescens

A great feature tree for small spaces located in dry sites. This tree has a very narrow, upright growth habit and produces yellow blooms in May. Height: 4–5m; width: 1m. Sun.

Cranberry 'American Highbush'
Viburnum trilobum

A large shrub—great for screening or as a fall accent plant. Large, flat clusters of white blooms appear in late spring, followed by masses of edible red berries. Foliage turns bright red in fall. Height: 3–4m; width: 3–4m. Sun to P.M. sun.

Lilac 'Beauty of Moscow'
Syringa vulgaris 'Krasavitsa Moskvy'

Considered by lilac experts to be one of the best bloomers, this large shrub makes an excellent screening plant or feature. It spreads and is a very heavy bloomer. Produces masses of fragrant, pink, double blooms in spring. Height: 3–4m; width: 2.5–3m. Sun to P.M. sun.

Cranberry 'American Highbush'

Caragana 'Sutherland'

Aspen 'Swedish Columnar'

Maple 'Sensation'
Acer negundo

An extremely hardy tree, featuring
bright green foliage with a pow-
dery-blue coating on the stems and
buds. Displays a slow, uniform growth
habit—perfect for smaller yards. Height:
7–10m; width: 6–7m. Sun.

Nannyberry
Viburnum lentago

This shrub produces lustrous, compact,
dark green foliage and creamy-white
blooms in June followed by edible,
blue-black fruits. Fruits are excellent
for jams and jellies. Prune after flowering. Height: 4–5m; width: 2–3m. Sun
or shade.

Ornamental Crabapple 'Rosthern Columnar (Siberian)'
Malus baccata 'Columnaris'

One of the most columnar flowering
crabapples. Makes a great feature tree
for small yards or addition to a mixed
screen. Covered in masses of white
blooms in May followed by yellow-
checkered red fruit. Height: 6m; width:
1.5–2m. Sun.

Pine 'Austrian'
Pinus nigra

An excellent, salt-tolerant evergreen
tree featuring very long, dark green

Maple 'Sensation'

Nannyberry

Ornamental Crabapple 'Rosthern Columnar'

needles—makes a good feature tree, screen or windbreak in dry areas. Shows a lot of character with age. Height: 20m; width: 7–10m. Sun.

Poplar 'Tower'
Populus x *canescens*

Stately screen or tall, semi-formal hedge, this tree is perfect for small yards and does not sucker. Fast-growing with an extremely upright growth habit. Height: 20m; width: 2–3m. Sun.

Willow 'Laurel Leaf'
Salix pentandra

A fast-growing and extremely hardy, large tree for open areas. Does well in moist sites and prevents soil erosion on banks. Produces very dark green, glossy foliage on an attractive form. Height: 10–15m; width: 7–10m. Sun.

Pine 'Austrian'

Poplar 'Tower'

Willow 'Laurel Leaf'

7

Architectural Influences

Beyond Your Control

Anyone who owns a home likes to think of himself as master of his domain, and creating an attractive landscape is an expression of not only ownership but artistry. Unfortunately, we can't control every aesthetic aspect of our gardening kingdom—within its boundaries or without. Much as it sometimes pains us, there is a zone of outside influence that cannot help but have an effect on our gardens—and that effect isn't always pleasant.

Your particular "canvas" may contain many challenges. It may be draped down a slope or over rocky terrain. Your home may have unattractive window wells or siding that's become unsightly, or a garage positioned right in the sunniest part of the yard. Challenges abound outside the yard as well. Overhead power lines, ugly fences built by the neighbours, dilapidated back alleys—these are the borderlands that chafe at any homeowner's desire to create the perfect yard. It's like framing the Mona Lisa with used two-by-fours.

Some of these outside influences can be changed only with great effort and expense; others are the proverbial immovable objects and must be worked around. The creativity and tenacity of gardeners who deal with such issues regularly amaze me. When the frame around your own little masterpiece is lacking, you just have to build a more appealing inner frame, a hedge or screen around the periphery of your yard. I used clematis, for example, to hide a particularly ugly fence on one side of my yard.

It's also important to remember that the world beyond your yard isn't static. As neighbours move and the community grows, the land surrounding your domain will change, sometimes looking better, sometimes worse. Be prepared for these changes, focusing on the content of your picture if you see something ugly brewing on the horizon.

Any artist worth his salt understands the limitations of his chosen form. For gardeners, the landscape itself can present daunting limitations…or endless opportunities. Flex your creative muscles, and you'll find that you can influence the landscape as much as it influences you.

IN THE GARDEN

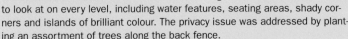

Penny and Dave Odegard's newly developed lot faced outside influences that created serious problems. The house sat at the bottom of a very steep hill, and the neighbouring homes further up the hill had a direct sightline into their yard, affording no privacy.

The Odegards purchased the lot well aware of these issues, but felt that with the right plan they could be overcome. They decided to divide the slope into terraces with carefully constructed retaining walls, along with paths and steps to allow access to each terrace. There is something to look at on every level, including water features, seating areas, shady corners and islands of brilliant colour. The privacy issue was addressed by planting an assortment of trees along the back fence.

Dave and Penny worked very hard to overcome some serious challenges, but the result is a yard that is far more interesting than your average flat space. Those outside influences looked daunting at first, but they pushed the Odegards to new creative heights.

This parking pad was given a new life as a patio, complete with framed beds used as a herb garden.

I have a parking pad made of interlocking stone in a hot, sunny area of my yard but no longer need it as we have built a garage elsewhere in our yard. I want to remove some of the discoloured stone to create small beds and use it as a patio. What grows here?

REMOVING THE STONE to create beds is the easy part. The difficult part is dealing with the compacted soil beneath the pavers. Soil compaction destroys soil structure; we've seen it often in our vegetable fields when tractor tires compress wet soil and plant roots can't penetrate it. Remove the pavers and the layer of sand that they are installed upon. If the driveway was layed on a clay base, remove some of that clay and replace it with topsoil. Because you are creating small beds, rototilling may not be an option. Instead, you may have to loosen the soil by hand and work in lots of organic matter. The depth you need to go will depend on what you choose to plant. If it's really tough going, you could frame the beds with landscape ties, raising them and filling each bed with good-quality loose soil. Because this area is sunny and very hot, it sounds like the perfect spot for a tidy heat-loving herb garden.

FRUIT

Strawberries 'Tri-Star'
Fragaria
Deliciously sweet, day-neutral strawberries producing high yields in July
to September. Enjoy fresh or processed.
Prefers moist, fertile soil. Height: 10cm;
spreads via runners. Sun.

HERBS

Lemongrass
Cymbopogon citrates
This versatile herb is useful for flavour-
ing fish, soups, curries and sauces, also
good for teas. Requires well-drained
soil. Height: 70–150cm; spacing: 60–
90cm. Sun.

Mint
Mentha spicata
Mint is an aggressively spreading plant
that is best suited to a contained location. Good for mint jelly and serving
with lamb, new potatoes, peas and
carrots. Prefers rich, moist soil but will
grow almost anywhere. Height: 60cm;
width: 60–90cm. Sun.

Oregano
Oregano 'Greek'
This herb blooms July to September
and can be pinched back to encourage
branching and bushy growth. Its hot,
spicy flavour complements almost all
tomato dishes, especially Italian cuisine.
Requires well-drained soil; roots will
rot if over-watered. Height: 30–60 cm;
width: 30–60cm. Sun.

Sage
Salvia officinalis 'Garden'
Salvia has fragrant, grey-green leaves
and blue flowers in June. This is the
most commonly grown variety—great
with poultry and pork. and excellent
in stuffing. Requires well-drained soil;
roots will rot if over-watered. Height:
45–90cm; spread: 1m. Sun.

Strawberries 'Tri-Star'

Sage 'Garden'

Oregano 'Greek'

Lemongrass

Unappealing structures, such as an ugly fence or shed, can be screened out with strategically positioned plants in a pleasing arrangement.

Our neighbour has erected a very ugly fence on his side of the property line. He is not willing to allow me to paint or modify it in any way, and as he owns it and it is on his land, I have no recourse. I'm thinking about screening it out with plants. What grows here?

SOMETIMES YOU SIMPLY can't reach an agreement on these types of issues with neighbours and it is best to just look for other solutions, as you have done. There are many plants that can grow to screen the unsightly fence or any other annoying features. You may choose to plant one variety (basically creating a living fence), to form a colourful border from many varieties or to construct a free-standing trellis that provides support for roses or vines. In my own yard I have planted twelve Techny cedars that are doing a great job of screening out my neighbour's fence. When I see how good these living barriers look, I wonder why people are still putting up wooden or metal fences at all.

ANNUALS

Castor Bean 'Green'

This tropical looking annual is useful as a fast-growing annual screen featuring large, deeply lobed, green foliage. Heat and drought tolerant. Height: up to 3m; spacing: 1–1.5m. Sun.

PERENNIALS

Big Petal Clematis

Clematis macropetala

Produces a lush, pest-free and very hardy screen that requires support. Grow as a climber, groundcover or trailing over stone walls. Do not cut back. Pink-mauve flowers in spring are followed by attractive seed heads. Prefers fertile, well-drained soil and cool roots. Height: 2–5m; width: 1–2m. Sun to P.M. sun.

Feather Reed Grass

Calamagrostis x *acutiflora* 'Karl Foerster'

One of the best clump forming grasses to grow as a feature plant in a mixed border (adds height). Light pink seed heads fade to tan in late summer. Leave stems in place for winter interest. Prefers moist, organic soil. Height: 90–150cm; width: 30–45cm. Sun to P.M. sun.

Feather Reed Grass 'Karl Foerster'

Castor Bean 'Green'

Big Petal Clematis

Golden Clematis
Clematis tangutica

Tanguticas are the largest, hardiest and most vigorous clematis. They climb on supports and also make great ground-covers for slopes or banks. Bright yellow, nodding bell flowers appear in late spring to fall followed by attractive seed heads. Prune back by one third in spring. Prefers well-drained soil and cool roots. Height: 4–5m; width: 2–3m. Sun to P.M. sun.

Golden Common Hops
Humulus lupulus 'Aureus'

This vigorous vine requires a strong support for its climbing habit and will cover a large area. Needs sun to keep its coarse, large foliage a bright golden colour. The female and male flowers are on separate plants. Cone-like, green, female flowers appear in summer. Prefers well-drained, organic, moderately fertile, moist soil. Height: 3–4m; width 2–3+m. Sun.

Roses

'Red Leaf Rose'
Species

A very hardy and pretty plant prized for its foliage, size and blooms. Striking reddish-purple foliage with a blue cast highlights clustered flowers in mid to late June. Single, mauve pink, 3–4cm flowers have a light fruity fragrance. Height: 1.5–2m; width: 1.5 m. Sun.

Golden Common Hops

'Red Leaf Rose'

Golden Clematis

'William Baffin' Explorer
Hybrid Kordesii

The hardiest climbing rose for Zone 2, featuring large clusters of up to 30 roses. Semi-double, red-pink with yellow-centered, 6–7cm flowers with a light fragrance bloom all summer. Height: 2–3m; width: 1.5–2m. Sun.

Lilac 'Charles Joly'
Syringa vulgaris

Good for informal hedges and screens—spreading habit. Produces masses of double, purple-red, fragrant blooms in spring. Height: 3m; width: 3m. Sun to P.M. sun.

TREES & SHRUBS

Cedar 'Techny' (Mission)
Thuja occidentalis

This hardy, slow-growing cedar makes a very attractive, dense living fence that is wind tolerant. Its dark green foliage, which looks coarse when young, is very tolerant of shearing and shaping. Height: 3–5m; width: 2m. Sun to P.M. sun.

Lilac 'Charles Joly'

'William Baffin' Rose

Cedar 'Techny'

Access ramps needn't be ugly nor obtrusive. Constructed as a graded sidewalk, this one is integrated into the landscape with well-positioned beds and attractive plants.

We have recently modified our home to make it barrier free for our son. A long, rather unattractive wooden wheelchair ramp has been installed leading to our door. We would like to integrate it into the yard. What grows here?

OFTEN IT IS THE GRADUATED HEIGHT, the length and the materials that access ramps are composed of that make them feel incongruent in a landscape, but that doesn't have to be the case. Recognize the ramp as an integral part of the architecture of your home, like the steps it has replaced, and paint or stain it to complement your exterior colour scheme. Soften the edges of it by planting along its sides with plants of graduated height, and with some that offer coverage in winter as well. Be vigilant about pruning any branches that protrude onto the ramp. Lastly, provide a destination feature at each end of the ramp: a lovely hanging basket by the door to your home or colourful planters mounted on the rails, and perhaps a bed with a statuary feature (at the other end). Just remember to leave room for easy movement.

ANNUALS

Lavatera 'Silver Cup'

These bushy plants produce satiny rose, cup-shaped flowers—very showy in the garden. Great in mass displays. Wind tolerant. Height: 60–90cm; spacing: 40–60cm. Sun.

Snapdragon 'Madame Butterfly'

Snapdragons are an old-fashioned favourite available in a wide range of colours and heights. Madame Butterfly has double, azalea-type flowers that give the appearance of a fuller, more graceful flower spike. Available as a mix. "Snaps" make a great cutflower. Height: 75cm; spacing: 25–30cm. Sun.

Sunflower 'Prado Red'

A medium-height sunflower that produces lots of striking, mahogany-red, 10–15cm, single flowers. Blooms make superb cutflowers. Height: 90–150cm; spacing: 45–60cm. Sun.

PERENNIALS

Cushion Spurge

Euphorbia polychroma

This spurge forms a neat mound and never spreads from its allotted space. Bright chartreuse-yellow bracts appear in spring. Tolerant of poor soil but it prefers well-drained, sandy soil in a hot and dry location. Height: 40–60cm; width: 40–60cm. Sun.

Lavatera 'Silver Cup'

Snapdragon 'Madame Butterfly'

Cushion Spurge

Sunflower 'Prado Red'

Daylily

Hemerocallis 'Stella D'oro'

Daylilies are hardy, versatile, clump-forming plants—ideal for any mixed border. They benefit from dividing every three to five years. This short daylily produces golden-yellow flowers continuously summer to fall. Fragrant flowers last longer than a single day. Prefers moist, fertile, well-drained soil. Height: 30cm; width: 30–60cm. Sun to P.M. sun.

Purple Bugbane

*Actea simplex (*syn. *Cimicifuga simplex* v. *simplex* or *C. ramosa)* 'Atropurpurea'

A striking feature plant. Purplish stems and foliage highlight fragrant, bottle-brush-like, white flowers on arching stems in fall. Clump-forming and upright in habit. Prefers moist, fertile, organic, cool soil in woodland location. Height: 1–1.5m; width: 60–90cm. Shade to A.M. sun.

TREES & SHRUBS

Lilac 'Charisma'

Syringa x *prestoniae*

Very attractive in borders or mass plantings, primarily grown for its very dense foliage. Excellent choice for informal hedges and is non-suckering. Produces fragrant, deep purple blooms in late May–June. Height: 75–90cm; width: 75–90cm. Sun.

Daylily 'Stella D'oro'

Lilac 'Charisma'

Purple Bugbane 'Atropurpurea'

Lilac 'Dwarf Korean'
Syringa meyeri 'Palibin'
This dwarf form of lilac makes a lovely hedge or feature shrub. Late each spring red-purple buds open to pink-purple, fragrant blooms on a non-suckering and compact plant. Height: 1–2m; width: 1.5–2m. Sun to P.M. sun.

Spiraea 'Little Princess'
Spiraea japonica
A small, rounded and compact form of spiraea that is attractive near the front to middle of borders. Fast growing with good red fall colour. Pretty bright pink blooms in summer. Height: 60–75cm; width: 90–100cm. Sun to P.M. sun.

Willow 'Blue Fox'
Salix brachycarpa
A compact willow that is great in foundation plantings and shrub beds. Features attractive blue-green foliage. Prefers moist soil. Height: 60–200cm; width: 60–200cm. Sun to P.M. sun.

Spiraea 'Little Princess'

Willow 'Blue Fox'

Lilac 'Dwarf Korean'

This 20-year-old Virginia Creeper reliably covers a home's facade year after year.

The front of our home is covered with old-fashioned, ugly stucco and, as we are not planning on re-siding it for a while, we'd like to cover it with plants. What grows here?

THERE ARE SEVERAL PLANTS that can offer temporary or permanent solutions. If you are planning on repairing or changing the offending stucco in the very near future, annual vines can be used. Another solution is to mount brackets and hang baskets of trailing annuals that dangle down and visually block the wall. If the stucco renovations won't take place for several years, fast-growing perennial vines and climbing roses can be used, but some may take a few years to establish well enough to provide satisfying coverage. Roses and vines require support in the form of trellis work or wire mounted to the wall. Of course, you also have the option of combining several kinds of plants, that is using the annual vines and baskets to fill in until the perennial vines and roses become sizeable enough to solve the problem on their own.

ANNUALS

Cup & Saucer Vine 'Purple'
Cobaea scandens

This fast-growing annual vine loves a warm sunny spot and is wind tolerant. Foliage is deep green with light green maturing to purple, large, cup-shaped flowers. Height: up to 3m; spacing: 25–30cm. Sun.

Petunia, Double Wave Series

This variety produces loads of 5–6cm, double flowers on a plant with a vigorous growth habit. Easily fills and spills over the sides of containers. Height: 25–40cm; spreads: to 60–90cm. Sun to P.M. sun.

Trailing Bamboo
Agrostitis stolonifera

This is a really interesting-looking annual to grow. It has a vigorous, bushy and trailing habit producing grass-like foliage. Keep moist at all times. Frost tolerant. Trails to 1.5m. Sun to P.M. sun.

PERENNIALS

Hybrid Clematis
Clematis 'Elsa Spath'

A dense climbing vine that requires support. Plant all hybrid clematis against a south or west, heated foundation for winter protection. Grow a plant or mulch at base to keep roots cool. Flowers open a rich blue shade and fade to mauve blue in summer. Prefers well-drained, fertile soil in a sheltered location. Height: 1.8–2m; width: 1–2m. Sun to P.M. sun.

Scarlet Trumpet Honeysuckle
Lonicera x *brownii*
'Dropmore Scarlet'

This easy to grow vine requires support to climb. Orange-scarlet flowers bloom early summer to fall and attract hummingbirds. Flowers are followed by red berries. Do not cut back in fall. Prefers well-drained, organic, moist soil but is somewhat tolerant of drought. Height: 4–6m; width 2–3+m. Sun to P.M. sun.

Virginia Creeper
Parthenocissus quinquefolia

This vine will easily cover a fence, wall or tree stump. Provide support for this vigorous climber. Ivy-like foliage turns brilliant red in fall. Green white flowers appear in summer followed by ornamental blue-black fruit. Do not cut back in fall. Prefers fertile, well-drained soil. Height: 5–10m; width: 2–3+m. Sun or shade.

Hybrid Clematis 'Elsa Spath'

Cup & Saucer Vine 'Purple'

Maggie Nielson, a staff member at our greenhouse, integrated a large garage into her landscape by using window boxes and a striking combination of perennials including bugbane, hosta, ferns and fleeceflower.

We have a very large, prominent and ugly garage in our backyard. We can't get rid of it, so it's been painted to complement the house and now we'd like to create a bed along its shady side to help it fit into the yard. What grows here?

SOMETIMES YOU SIMPLY CAN'T HIDE a utilitarian structure. A trick landscape designers use to integrate structures into the landscape involves repeating plantings that already exist in the general area. For example, if a wide, curvy foundation bed filled with colourful plants surrounds the back of your home, repeat that pattern along the garage. If the light conditions are very different and it is impossible to use the same plants, then choose different species with similar forms. Repeat the colour combinations and the size of the bed in proportion to the building. Even little touches like window boxes on a garage will help to unite it visually with the house.

ANNUALS

Begonia, Non Stop Series

This series offers non-stop colour. Beautiful, large, double flowers are displayed on a plant with a mounding habit. Excellent in hanging baskets, containers and flowerbeds. Height: 20–25cm; spacing: 15–25cm. Shade to A.M. sun.

Impatiens, Dazzler Series

Impatiens are the annual workhorses of the shade garden, providing consistent bright colour to dark areas. This series displays masses of 4cm, single flowers in many shades. Height: 20–25cm; spacing: 10–15cm. Shade to A.M. sun.

Goat's Beard 'Kneiffii'

PERENNIALS

American Alumroot
Heuchera americana 'Velvet Night'

Heucheras are hardy plants that are prized for their attractive foliage and tiny blooms. Clump-forming in habit, this variety displays metallic purple foliage over a slate-black underlay and tiny, cream flowers on 65cm stalks in midsummer. Prefers moist, fertile, well-drained soil. Height: 20cm; width: 45cm. Shade to A.M. sun.

Goat's Beard
Aruncus dioicus 'Kneiffii'

This clump-forming perennial has finely-cut foliage and plumes of cream flowers in spring. Foliage turns a fiery red in fall. Grow in a woodland garden with other shade-loving plants. Prefers moist, fertile soil. Height: 60–90cm; width: 60–90cm. Shade to A.M. sun.

Begonia 'Non Stop Rose-pink'

American Alumroot 'Velvet Night' and Goldleaf Bleeding Heart 'Goldheart' (featured on page 97).

Hosta
Hosta tsushimensis
(Tsushima Giboshi)

This hosta is found all over the island of Tsushima, which lies in the Korean Strait. An attractive, medium, dense mound of wavy green leaves with purple flowers in summer. Prefers moist, fertile, well-drained, organic, slightly acidic soil. Height: 30cm; width: 80cm. Shade to A.M. sun.

Narrow Spike Rayflower
Ligularia 'The Rocket'

Large leaves with black stems on this clump-forming, upright plant offer a hot tropical look for the garden. Spiked, bright yellow flowers bloom in summer. Avoid bright, windy sites. Requires very moist, deep, moderately fertile soil. Height: 1.2–1.8m; width: 75–90cm. Shade to A.M. sun.

Variegated Heartleaf Forget-Me-Not
Brunnera macrophylla 'Jack Frost'

This is a lovely colony-forming plant that is well used as a groundcover in a woodland site or in a shady border. Forget-me-not, blue flowers appear in spring above heart-shaped, silvery-green foliage. Prefers moist, well-drained, fertile, organic soil. Height: 35cm; width: 45–60cm. Shade to A.M. sun.

Variegated Heartleaf Forget-Me-Not 'Jack Frost'   *Narrow Spike Rayflower 'The Rocket'*

Hosta tsushimensis

Trees & Shrubs

Cedar 'Little Giant'
Thuja occidentalis 'Little Giant'
This somewhat columnar cedar is a
nice addition to a shady border, rock
garden or used as a formal hedge. It
features lovely, dense, medium green
foliage. Height: 100cm; width: 45–
60cm. A.M. sun.

Hydrangea 'Annabelle'
Hydrangea arborescens
A showy shrub with incredibly large,
white, ball-like blooms in August/Sept-
ember. Should be cut down to ground
in early spring. Requires moist soil.
Height: 60–90cm; width: 60–90cm.
Sun to A.M. sun.

Snowberry
Symphoricarpos albus
An undemanding native plant useful
in foundation plantings and informal
hedges. A great shrub for shady sites.
Features blue-green foliage and pink
blooms in late spring. Prune annually
to maintain compact form. Height:
90–100cm; width: 90–100cm. Sun or
shade.

Cedar 'Little Giant'

Hydrangea 'Annabelle'

Snowberry

Brighten up a long expanse of driveway with colourful combinations of annuals such as geraniums and dusty miller.

My driveway stretches from the street to the garage located in the rear of the backyard and is joined with our neighbour's, giving the impression of one vast sea of unappealing concrete. The area is sunny and very hot. What grows here?

DON'T THINK DRIVEWAY—think patio. This situation calls for a little ingenuity, presented here in varying degrees of difficulty. To break up the large expanse of concrete, simply run a narrow line of attractive pots filled with colourful annuals up the middle (but still on your side) of the driveway. Take this solution to the next level by constructing several long, narrow rectangular planters that can be placed directly between the driveways and removed at the end of each season. Make them tall enough to be visible when backing out of the driveway and give your back a break by mounting them on rolling casters with brakes. Perhaps your neighbours will be willing to share a portion of their side of the driveway to accommodate a wider mobile planter. Be sure to fill the pots and planters with good-quality potting soil and, as conditions are hot and sunny, be prepared to water often.

ANNUALS

Bidens 'Peter's Gold Carpet'

Excellent in hanging baskets, planters, or as an annual groundcover producing bright yellow, single flowers on lace-like green foliage. Height: 25–35cm; trails to 60cm. Sun.

Geranium, Designer Series

The Designer series offers many rich colours with extra large, double flowers that make them an appealing accent plant—excellent in containers, flowerbeds and hanging baskets. Height: 30–35cm; spacing; 30–35cm. Sun to P.M. sun.

Lantana, Landmark Series

Lantana are extremely heat-tolerant annuals that offer highly fragrant foliage that smells like lemony-sage. Dense clusters of flowers bloom in many shades—attracts hummingbirds. Height: 35–50cm; spread: 60cm. Sun.

Pennisetum 'Orientale'

Silky white, foxtail-like flowers wave atop an arching clump of glossy, blue-green foliage. Ideal feature plant. Heat and drought tolerant. Height: 60–90cm; spacing: 45–75cm. Sun to P.M. sun.

Petunia, Easy Wave Series

This series produces loads of colourful, 5cm, double flowers on a plant with a vigorous mounding habit. Excellent garden performance and weather tolerance. Easily fills and spills over the sides of containers. Height: 15cm; spreads: to 90cm. Sun to P.M. sun.

ROSES

'Carefree Wonder'
Tender Shrub

A showy, award-winning rose that does very well in a container. Considered hardy to Zone 4, it displays double, medium pink with light pink undersides, 7–8cm flowers with a light fragrance from June to frost. Height: 1m; width: 1m. Sun.

Bidens 'Peter's Gold Carpet'

'Carefree Wonder' Rose

Pennisetum 'Orientale'

Lantana 'Landmark Peach Sunrise'

'Hansa' rose makes a very pretty barrier grown in front of a raised window.

The windows on the side of our home are very accessible to an adjacent public walkway and I want to place thorny plants next to the sidewalk to create an attractive physical boundary. The area is hot and sunny. What grows here?

YOU MAY NOT NEED a living barbed wire fence to keep people at a respectful distance. Make sure that you determine the severity of the problem first, and then choose your plants. Tall, non-barbed plants such as cedars may be enough to do the trick, and might be more aesthetically appealing than some prickly choices. A thorny barrier may well discourage anyone from trying to access your windows, but be sure that it doesn't stop you from being able to maintain or open them, especially in the case of an emergency. If you are interested in instant results, purchase big plants, although they will be more expensive.

ROSES

'Hansa' Shrub
Hybrid Rugosa

One of the best all-round rugosas. This variety is very long-lived and hardy to Zone 1. It produces double, fuchsia-red, 8–10cm flowers with a strong clove-like fragrance in June or July and repeating all summer. Height; 1.5–2m; width: 1.5–2m. Sun.

'Martin Frobisher' Explorer
Hybrid Rugosa

This pillar-shaped shrub has erect canes and reddish bark. It is hardy to Zone 2. Double, soft pink, 5–6cm flowers with a light fragrance bloom profusely all summer. Height: 2m; width: 2m. Sun.

TREES & SHRUBS

Barberry 'Cherry Bomb'
Berberis thunbergii var. *atropurpurea* 'Monomb'

Deep crimson-coloured foliage highlights this slow-growing, compact form. Bright yellow flowers appear in May/June. Height: 90–100cm; width: 90–100cm. Sun.

Cedar 'Boisbriand'
Thuja occidentalis

This cedar sports dense, dark green foliage on an egg-shaped form that is useful for screening. Annual shearing helps to maintain its compact shape. Height: 3m; width: 1.5–2m. Sun to P.M. sun.

Lilac 'Miss Canada'
Syringa x *prestoniae*

This is a very nice, non-suckering variety of lilac developed in Canada. It produces large hanging clusters of magenta, single blooms in early summer. Height: 3m; width: 3m. Sun to P.M. sun.

Spiraea 'Dwarf Garland'
Spiraea x *arguta* 'Compacta'

An excellent shrub for use as a feature in beds and borders. White blooms smother long, slender arching branches before or as the leaves appear in late spring—very showy. Height: 1m; width: 1m. Sun to P.M. sun.

Spiraea 'Dwarf Garland'

Lilac 'Miss Canada'

'Martin Frobisher' Rose

Trailing plants grown outside a window well will spill over its edges and disguise the walls without blocking precious light into the basement.

Our new home has large basement windows surrounded by unattractive concrete window wells that are wide and deep. I want to improve the view looking out from these windows but I don't want to block the light and I'm considering planting in the well itself. What grows here?

M ANY NEW HOMES are designed with bigger basement windows to gain interior light and for safety. These windows are surrounded by large wells made of concrete or metal and are filled at the bottom with gravel that drains water away from the window. Plants won't grow well in this deep gravel and careless watering could cause water damage to the window sill. Also you shouldn't block any window that could serve as an emergency escape route. With these points in mind, try one of these approaches. Place a small container of shade annuals in the well, on top of the gravel, provided it will receive enough light, that you water carefully and that the wndow can be opened. Or, outside the well, place trailing plants that will eventually spill over the upper edge and help to disguise the walls. The final solution doesn't involve plants at all: position a small piece of statuary in the well (again not blocking escape) or hang a decorative plaque on the well wall to improve the view.

ANNUALS

Black-Eyed Susan Vine 'Alata Mix'

This pretty annual vine displays curling tendrils, heart-shaped foliage and open-faced, trumpet-shaped flowers with black centres in a mix of orange, yellow and cream. Grow up a trellis or netting or allow to spill over an edge. Height: 1m; spacing: 10–15cm. Sun.

Calibrachoa, Million Bells Series

A fast-growing, heavy-blooming and self-cleaning plant that thrives in hanging baskets, containers or grown as an annual groundcover. Produces small petunia-like, bright blooms in several shades. Height: 8–15cm; trails: 45–60cm. Sun.

Vinca 'Green & Gold'

Vinca maculatum

This plant offers bright green and gold variegated foliage, often with lilac flowers. A superb contrast plant with a very vigorous trailing habit. Trails to 1–1.5m. Sun to P.M. sun.

TREES & SHRUBS

Juniper 'Wilton's Blue Rug'

Juniperus horizontalis 'Wiltonii'

A very hardy and fast-growing juniper with trailing branches and silver-blue foliage that is tinged purple in winter—very attractive trailing over wall edges. Extremely tolerant of hard soil. Height: 10–15cm; width: 2–3m. Sun.

Mahonia 'Creeping Mahonia'

Mahonia repens

Suitable for mass plantings in low light areas. Dark green, evergreen foliage highlights small black fruits in late August. Foliage turns purple in fall. Requires snow cover. Height: 30cm; width: 60cm. Shade to A.M. sun.

Russian Cypress

Microbiota decussata

A great groundcover that spreads indefinitely in the right conditions. We know of a 14-year-old shrub that was four meters wide! Bright green foliage turns purple-brown in winter. Requires moist soil. Height: 30cm; width: 3–4m. Shade to A.M. sun.

Russian Cypress

Mahonia 'Creeping Mahonia'

Calibrachoa 'Million Bells Trailing Pink'

Vinca 'Green & Gold'

Turn an ugly, utilitarian swale into a landscape feature by softening its edges with plants and rocks designed to create the look and feel of a dry creek.

We have a concrete swale that cannot be removed running through our backyard. It looks so odd! We're really not very enthusiastic gardeners, but we do want to try to integrate it into the yard with low–maintenance, permanent plantings. What grows here?

SWALES ARE CREATED to direct water flow not only in one yard, but in some cases through an entire block. They tend to be constructed in a very linear manner and do look utilitarian and odd. An easy way to blend this type of utility into a landscape is to create a border on either side and fill it with plants that will arch up and trail over the swale's sides, softening its edges. This border can run parallel with the swale or it could curve in a snake-like manner with the swale running up its centre. Enhance the area with a bridge spanning the swale and place decorative rock along its edges, being careful not to block its drainage function. These extra steps will help to make it appear more of a feature than an eyesore.

PERENNIALS

Blue Fescue
Festuca glauca
A wonderful clump-forming accent plant to use with evergreens. Blue-green foliage produces blue-green seed heads in summer. Prefers well-drained, dry soil. Height: 25–40cm; width: 25–30cm. Sun to P.M. sun.

Daylily
Hemerocallis 'Chicago Apache'
Daylilies are hardy, versatile, clump-forming plants with grass-like foliage that are ideal for any mixed border. They benefit from dividing every three to five years. Ruffled, deep scarlet flowers appear in late spring to late summer. Prefers moist, fertile, well-drained soil. Height: 70cm; width: 45–75cm. Sun to P.M. sun.

Serbian Bellflower
Campanula poscharskyana 'Blue Waterfall'
This pretty plant has a vigorous spreading habit that is good for banks, wild gardens or rock gardens. Attractive blue flowers appear in summer to fall. Prefers fertile, well-drained, moist soil. Height: 8–15cm; width: 30–60cm. Sun to P.M. sun.

TREES & SHRUBS

Birch 'Trost Dwarf'
Betula tianschanica
Well suited to larger rock gardens, this interesting shrub drapes over rocks and overhangs very nicely. Thread-like leaves are displayed on a compact, slow-growing plant. Prefers rich, moist, acidic soil. Height: 90–150cm; width: 90–150cm. Sun to P.M. sun.

Juniper 'Calgary Carpet'
Juniperus sabina 'Monna'
This low-growing, spreading and very popular juniper has soft green foliage and a tolerance to light shade. Prefers dry soil. Height: 20–30cm; width: 2–3m. Sun.

Stephanandra 'Cutleaf'
Stephanandra incisa 'Crispa'
A finely textured, compact groundcover with reddish-bronze new foliage that turns reddish-orange again in the fall. Lovely spilling over rocks and it roots where branches touch the soil—great on slopes. Height: 30–60cm; width: 100–200cm. Sun to P.M. sun.

Juniper 'Calgary Carpet'

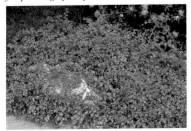

Stephanandra 'Cutleaf'

Blue Fescue

Many columnar junipers, such as 'Moonglow', can be used under power lines to provide privacy but be sure to check with local authorities for height restrictions.

We would like to gain some privacy on the street side of our yard and want to plant a row of trees to serve this purpose. However, a power line runs overhead along the length of our property. What grows here?

IT IS REALLY WISE to consider the full-grown height of trees when selecting a variety that will be planted near power lines. Over the years we've seen and heard of a lot of trees that have had to be trimmed or even removed because they posed a hazard. This situation can leave the gardener with a very unattractive tree or a major space to fill in the mature landscape. Always consult your local power company for the guidelines for allowable heights of trees in your area. Trees or large shrubs that reach no more than six to seven metres tall can usually be safely used. That being said, a mixed bed of interesting large shrubs can offer privacy without concern for height restrictions.

Elder 'Golden Plume'
Sambucus racemosa 'Plumosa Aurea'
This vigorous shrub offers finely textured gold foliage that provides excellent contrast in a mixed shrub bed.
White blooms in spring are followed
by red fruit in summer. Height: 1.5–
3m; width: 1.5–3m. Sun to P.M. sun.

Juniper 'Moonglow'
Juniperus scopulorum
Intense bluish-grey foliage on a dense,
pyramidal form—great as a feature
plant or planted in a group as a hardy
screen. Height: 6m; width: 1.5m. Sun.

Lilac 'James MacFarlane'
Syringa x *prestoniae*
This lilac is non-suckering, providing
a screen of dark green foliage with
masses of rich pink, single blooms in
spring. Height: 3–4m; width: 3–4m.
Sun to P.M. sun.

Maple 'Tatarian'
Acer tataricum
This is a beautiful small tree for use in
small yards that produces red-winged
seeds in August and deep red and
orange fall colour. Blooms in May
prior to leafing out. Height: 5–6m;
width: 5–6m. Sun to P.M. sun.

Wayfaring Tree 'Mohican'
Viburnum lantana
This compact form is great for screening. Deep green leaves turn purple-red
in fall and creamy-white blooms in
May are very pretty. Height: 2–3m;
width: 2–3 m. Sun.

Willow 'Polar Bear'
Salix silicola
This hardy shrub has lots of pussy
willows in spring followed by silver-
white and blue, furry foliage—great
for colour and texture contrast. Prefers
moist soil. Height: 3m; width: 3m. Sun.

Elder 'Golden Plume'

Juniper 'Moonglow'

Willow 'Polar Bear'

8

Water

The Essential Element

This planet has plenty of water, but it won't do your plants any good if it's in the wrong place. Part of your job as a gardener is to ensure that each plant in your yard gets the correct share of the good stuff. By weight, water is the largest single component of any plant. So it should come as no surprise that management of this essential resource is critical for plant survival, let alone healthy growth.

Too often, we look at plants in isolation, designating a plant as a heavy or light user of water, without taking into account the dramatic effect that other factors have on water use—the simplest factor being your ability to get water to your plants when they need it. Hostas are perhaps the most famous of the shade plants, but they will do surprisingly well in full sun—if (and only if) you keep them consistently moist. Damage to shade plants such as hostas is often attributed to intense sunlight, but the truth is most of the damage occurs because hostas close their stomata (leaf pores) when they're not absorbing enough water through their roots to make up for the water lost through their leaves. These closed pores also stop the plant from transpiring—that is, giving off excess heat. The foliage can't cool off. When the leaf temperature rises excessively, cells die and the leaves develop brown patches. The lesson is that you can create a problem for yourself, and the plant, if you don't consider the plant's need for water and your ability to deliver it.

Our yards are miniature versions of our planet, including areas where water pools and places where there seems to be no soil moisture at all. Make life easier by determining where and how water is distributed in your yard, and plant accordingly. That boggy patch at the end of the garden is a prime spot for water-loving plants. As for the bone-dry patch under the front window, either grow drought-tolerant plants or be prepared to provide the extra water they'll need to grow well outside their ideal environment.

IN THE GARDEN

Chris and Jim Newton knew that distributing water effectively to their plants was going to be a challenge.

The stone retaining walls they used to fix an extreme grading problem held in heat, dramatically raising temperatures in the yard, and redirected water flow; some areas were now desert-like hot zones and others cool, very moist, shady spots. It became apparent that if they were going to garden successfully, they had to carefully address the water needs of every plant they selected.

The Newtons made sure that the dry areas were amended with moisture-retaining organic matter. Chris planted trees in the really hot spots to provide future shade, and while waiting for the trees to grow larger (and carefully keeping them watered), she planted drought-tolerant plants that could handle the retained heat of the stone. The cool, moist, shady spots were addressed with selections that thrived in these conditions.

By understanding how water was distributed in their yard and determining the individual water needs of each of their plants, Chris and Jim created a lush, thriving garden—without wasting precious water.

Once well-established, many plants have minimal watering needs, but don't count on eliminating watering completely from your gardening routine.

Our very sunny front yard is quite dry most of the year and when we are away for an entire month at a time in the summer, we have to hire someone to keep the yard watered. We have decided to redesign our yard to eliminate watering altogether. What grows here?

A LOT OF PEOPLE TRAVEL during our short summers and having a landscape that is somewhat self-sustaining can make being away much simpler. Of course, it is also easier on the pocketbook in terms of saving watering and maintenance costs. Unfortunately, your desire to eliminate watering entirely probably won't give you a garden that you will be aesthetically pleased with. There are plants that will survive with nothing but rainfall, but they may not perform to their true potential. Many drought-tolerant plants endure dry spells by virtually shutting down growth, resulting in some pretty haggard-looking plants. You're far better off to compromise by considering wise water use and selecting plants that can perform well under drier conditions but require just a few hard waterings per year. Reduce watering by mulching beds to slow water loss and to keep the soil cool. Consider that many plants require a bit of nurturing to become established, and during drought years or very hot summers the garden may need supplemental watering.

Annuals

Amaranthus 'Love Lies Bleeding'
Amaranthus caudatus

A superb feature plant that is quite striking in backgrounds. Long, dark red and trailing rope-like flowers make interesting cut or dried flowers. Drought tolerant once established. Height: 90–150cm; spacing: 35–45cm. Sun.

Gazania, Daybreak Series

A heat-loving annual that thrives in dry borders and rock gardens. This series produces 10cm, daisy-like flowers in orange, yellow, pink and white. Heat and drought tolerant. Height: 20–25cm; spacing: 15–20cm. Sun.

Fall Bulbs

Species Tulip
Tulipa tarda

This pretty species tulip produces fragrant, star-shaped, bright yellow flowers with white tips in mid spring. Seed pods are attractive. Multiplies readily by stolons. Requires well-drained, gravelly soil. Height: 12–15cm: plant 12–20cm deep and 12–15cm apart. Sun to P.M. sun.

Gazania, Daybreak Series

Amaranthus 'Love Lies Bleeding'

Tulipa tarda

PERENNIALS

Adam's Needle
Yucca filamentosa

Valued for its bold, upright form. Produces dark green foliage edged with curly, white thread—do not cut back. White flowers tinged yellow appear in summer. Does best in a sheltered site away from cold, drying winds. Prefers well-drained soil—avoid winter wet. Height: 60–75cm; width: 60–100cm. Sun.

Brome Grass
Bromus inermis 'Skinner's Gold'

This grass with bright green and gold foliage produces very ornamental seed heads in summer. Makes a great groundcover or background for other perennials, but it should be planted in a contained area, as it will spread. Cut back in the heat of summer to create fresh new growth. Prefers fertile soil. Height: 60–90cm; width: 60+cm. Sun.

Catmint
Nepeta racemosa (syn. *N. mussinii*)

This long-blooming, drought-tolerant plant brightens up any mixed border with spikes of violet-purple flowers from midsummer to fall. Prefers well-drained soil. It has a spreading, upright habit and mint-scented foliage. Height: 30cm; width: 30–45cm. Sun to P.M. sun.

Brome Grass 'Skinner's Gold'

Adam's Needle

Catmint

Flat Sea Holly

Eryngium planum

A very attractive plant that may be used for naturalizing or as an accent. Evergreen foliage produces small, blue flowers in midsummer to fall that make excellent dried flowers. Drought and salt tolerant. Requires well-drained, dry soil. Clump-forming in habit. Height: 75–90cm; width: 45cm. Sun.

Western Sage

Artemisia ludoviciana
'Valerie Finnis'

Thriving in a hot and dry location, this clump-forming perennial displays silver-grey foliage with sharply cut edges—excellent accent plant. Does best in well-drained, alkaline, poor, dry soil. Height: 45–60cm; width: 60+cm. Sun to P.M. sun.

Western Sage 'Valerie Finnis'

TREES & SHRUBS

Caragana 'Pygmy'

Caragana pygmaea

A very good choice for hot, dry locations, this naturally vase-shaped form is excellent for small formal hedges. Produces tiny yellow flowers in late spring. Height: 1m; width: 1m. Sun to P.M. sun.

Genista 'Dwarf' (Lydia)

Genista lydia

An excellent groundcover plant for hot, dry areas producing masses of striking yellow blooms that last three to five weeks on a low-growing and spreading shrub. Height: 45–60cm; width: 90–100cm. Sun.

Flat Sea Holly

Genista 'Dwarf'

Drainage issues are solved in these two yards by sharing a "creek" that serves to direct excess run-off into the street sewer system.

Our newer neighbourhood has a high water table and we run a sump pump that drains out into the area between my garage and my neighbour's garage. The builder positioned the downspouts to drain into this spot as well. It is turning into a soggy mess. What grows here?

THE DRAINAGE ISSUE is important because water may leak into your home. The water from the sump pump itself may have high salt levels, which creates more than drainage problems. Direct the run-off into the city sewer system by grading the soil away from the foundation of each building and create a channel for the water to flow to the street. One attractive and functional solution is to install a "creek" using gravel and rock in an assortment of sizes. Position plants along the creek's edges for an appealing, natural look. Talk to your neighbour—perhaps you can work together to improve the situation, sharing the space and costs.

Spring Bulb

Canna Lily 'Phasion'

This tender bulb produces striking orange, red and green zebra-striped foliage with salmon-orange flowers—a superb feature plant. Lift the bulb in fall to overwinter. Height: up to 1m. Sun.

Perennials

Bowles' Golden Sedge

Carex elata 'Aurea'

Sedges are valued mainly for their grass-like leaves and 'Aurea' is one of the best golden sedges. Clump-forming in habit with arching, brilliant yellow foliage and flower spikes that appear in late spring to early summer. Thrives in fertile, moist, wet soil. Height: 45–60cm; width: 45cm. Sun to P.M. sun.

Dwarf Bearded Iris

Iris versicolor

This hardy iris produces pretty light blue flowers in late spring. Prefers alkaline-free, wet, organic soil. Clump-forming in habit. Height: 20–25cm; width: 30–45cm. Sun to P.M. sun.

Japanese Iris

Iris ensata 'Laughing Lion'

A great plant for a boggy area. Double, purplish-red flowers appear in early summer. Thrives in wet, acidic, organic soil. Clump-forming in habit. Height: 90cm; width: 45–60cm. Sun to P.M. sun.

Dwarf Bearded Iris

Canna Lily 'Phasion'

Japanese Iris 'Laughing Lion'

Martagon Lily
Lilium martagon 'Gay Lights'

A tall, elegant lily that produces abundant blooms of recurved, yellow-brown flowers with maroon spots in early summer. Requires cool, well-drained, moist, organic, soil. Height: 1.2–1.5m; width: 30–45cm. Sun to P.M. sun.

Willow Amsonia
Amsonia tabernaemontana

A really pretty, unusual plant for the edge of a woodland garden or border. Willow-like foliage highlights pale blue flowers that appear in late spring to midsummer. Prefers well-drained, moist soil but will tolerate some drought.

Clump-forming in habit. Height: 40–60cm; width: 30–45cm. Sun to P.M. sun.

TREES & SHRUBS

Birch 'Young's Weeping'
Betula pendula 'Youngii'

A strongly weeping tree that needs training to achieve a specific height, at which point it will weep down and may even cover the ground. This species is often grafted on a 1.5–2.5m single stem—a beautiful feature tree for small yards. Produces catkins in spring, bright white bark is attractive in all seasons and the branches are lovely covered in frost. Height: training dependant. Sun.

Birch 'Young's Weeping'

Willow Amsonia

Martagon Lily 'Gay Lights'

Hemlock 'Weeping'
Tsuga canadensis 'Gracilis'

This very attractive evergreen is low maintenance, needing no pruning. Graceful, weeping branches are very attractive in a rock garden. Requires moist soil. Height: 20–25cm; width: 40–50cm. A.M. sun.

Maple 'Bailey Compact'
Acer tataricum ssp. *ginnala*

This compact variety of maple is terrific for small yards and for screening. Foliage turns bright red in fall. Thrives in moist soil. Height: 2–3m; width: 2–3m. Sun to P.M. sun.

Willow 'Dwarf Arctic Blue Leaf'
Salix purpurea 'Nana'

A compact form of willow with light grey bark and deep blue foliage—great for contrast in shrub beds. Try it as an informal hedge. Prefers moist soil. Height: 1–1.5m; width: 1–1.5m. Sun.

Willow 'Dwarf Arctic Blue Leaf'

Maple 'Bailey Compact'

Hemlock 'Weeping'

Stephen Raven, our mailorder manager, has a lovely bed along a shady, damp side of his home that features plants such as glaucidium and hosta.

We have a very wet side yard that is also quite shady. The drainage in the area is not very good and the soil is compacted. I'm prepared to dig up this small area and make beds with a path winding between them. What grows here?

WET, COMPACTED SOIL is very difficult for most plants and the fact that this area is shady means that it may remain consistently moist. These areas also often remain quite cool, even in the height of summer. There can be no two ways about this situation: you have to improve the drainage if you are going to grow anything successfully. Roll up your sleeves and either dig up the soil (amending it with lots of organic matter) or build raised beds atop the area (filling them with a loose growing medium such as potting soil that drains quickly). This is a lot of work, but it will pay off in the years to come and give you another area of your yard to enjoy. These moist, shady conditions are perfect for a woodland garden!

PERENNIALS

Glaucidium
Glaucidium palmatum

A striking, slow-growing, large-leaved perennial for shady spots. Performs best in cool, moist areas—grow in a woodland garden. Lavender-blue flowers in early summer. Clump-forming in habit. Prefers moist, organic, well-drained soil. Protect from cold, drying winds. Height: 40–50cm; width: 45cm. Shade to A.M. sun.

False Solomon's Seal
Smilacina racemosa

Clump-forming with a slow, spreading habit. Arching foliage has fragrant cream flowers that appear in late spring followed by red berries. May go summer dormant if the location is too dry. Prefers organic, acidic, moist, well-drained soil. Height: 60–90cm; width: 45–60cm. Shade to A.M. sun.

Hosta
Hosta 'Sum and Substance'

One of the largest hostas—quite slug-resistant. Thick, lemon-green, cupped foliage produces lavender flowers in summer—needs some sun for best colour. Prefers moist, fertile, well-drained, organic, slightly acidic soil. Height: 75cm; width: 1.5+m. Shade to A.M. sun.

Kinnikinnik
Arctostaphylos uva-ursi

Shiny, evergreen foliage with a spreading habit makes a great groundcover. White to soft pink flowers in spring, followed by red, ornamental berries in the fall. Drought tolerant once established. Prefers moist, well-drained, acidic, fertile soil. Height: 10–15cm; width: 45–60cm. Sun to P.M. sun.

Korean Goat's Beard
Aruncus aethusifolius

Use as a groundcover in a woodland garden or shady border. Creamy-white plumes in spring to early summer are highlighted against finely textured foliage. Pretty fall colour. Prefers moist, fertile soil. Clump-forming, compact habit. Height: 30–40cm; width: 45–60cm. Shade to A.M. sun.

TREES & SHRUBS

Dogwood 'Siberian Pearls'
Cornus alba

Dark green foliage turns a rich reddish-purple in fall. Small white blooms in spring are followed by masses of pearly white berries on deep red stems that provide winter interest. Height: 2–3m; width: 2–3m. Sun to P.M. sun.

Korean Goat's Beard

Kinnikinnik

False Solomon's Seal

Colleen Jackson's beautiful pond's edges are softened with moisture-loving shrubs and grasses.

The flowerbed next to my pond remains quite moist, even though it is in full sun. Some of the plants we have placed there have actually rotted and I'm getting a little frustrated. I thought plants needed lots of water if they were in full sun! What grows here?

GARDENING SHOULD BE FUN, not frustrating and your frustration stems from using the wrong plants for this site. Match the plant to the site and you'll be back on track. Perhaps the area next to your pond is not just moist but wet, despite the fact that it is in full sun. Few plants love wet conditions because they are unable to access the oxygen and nutrients they require from sodden soil. The good news is that some plants will thrive in bog-like conditions. Check out the edge of a marsh in your area and you will see a host of grasses and flowering perennials and even some moisture-loving trees and shrubs. Look for plants at your local garden centre identified as marginals, so named because they live on the margins of bodies of water.

Spring Bulbs

Canna Lily
'Pretoria' (Bengal Tiger)
Canna

This tender bulb produces brilliant melon coloured flowers and yellow and green striped foliage—a superb feature plant. Requires a regular supply of moisture and a warm location. Lift the bulb in fall to overwinter. Height: up to 1m. Sun.

Perennials

Chinese Rhubarb
Rheum palmatum 'Atrosanguineum' (syn. *Atropurpureum*)

Great addition to a moist border, woodland garden or around a pond. Clump-forming in habit, with deeply lobed, palmate foliage that requires at least full A.M. sun to maintain deep colour. Leaves are crimson-red when young and the summer flower spikes are crimson-red. Prefers moist, organic, deep soil. Tolerates full sun if planted in cool, moist soil. Height: 2–2.5m; width: 1.2–1.8m. Sun to A.M. sun.

Golden Creeping Jenny
Lysimachia nummularia 'Aurea'

Use as a groundcover, even in wet areas, on slopes and in poor soil. Roots as it creeps along the top of the soil. Yellow-green foliage dislpays yellow flowers in late spring to summer. Prefers organic, moist, well-drained soil. Height: 2–5cm; width: 45–60+cm. Sun or shade.

Canna Lily 'Pretoria'

Chinese Rhubarb

Golden Creeping Jenny

Siberian Iris
Iris sibirica

One of the least demanding irises, this long-lived perennial thrives around ponds and is well suited to Japanese gardens. Clump-forming with sword-like foliage and pretty beardless flowers in late spring. Cut back in fall. Prefers well-drained, moist, slightly acidic soil. Height: 60cm; width: 30–45cm. Sun to P.M. sun.

Sweet Joe Pye
Eupatorium purpureum

A showy perennial that forms a large, clump-forming, upright bush—contrasts well with evergreens and attracts butterflies. Fragrant, clustered, rose-purple flowers bloom late in summer to fall. Prefers moist, alkaline soil. Height: 90–150cm; width: 90–150cm. Sun to P.M. sun.

Umbrella Plant
Darmera peltata

This interesting plant thrives in moist, boggy soil but tolerates dry periods. It has a slow, spreading habit and produces large, rounded, dark green leaves that turn red in fall. White to pink flowers appear in early spring. Height: 60–90cm; width: 60–90+cm. Sun to P.M. sun.

TREES & SHRUBS

Arrowwood
Viburnum dentatum

This durable hardy plant is an excellent choice for wet soils. Deep-green glossy foliage highlights white, flat-topped blooms in June, followed by black fruit that attracts birds. Can be grown singly, sheared as a hedge or used as a screen.

Hydrangea 'Pee Gee'

Siberian Iris

Height: 3–5m; width: 3–5m. Sun to
P.M. sun.

Elder 'Black Beauty'
Sambucus nigra 'Gerda'

An excellent plant for contrast—holds
dark purple foliage colour well.
Produces clustered pink, sweet lemon-
scented blooms in June followed by
black berries. Vigorous growth is easily
shaped. Height: 2–3m; width: 2–3m.
Sun to P.M. sun.

Hydrangea 'Pee Gee'
Hydrangea paniculata 'Grandiflora'

This shrub can grow much larger
depending on climate. Produces huge,
lovely pinkish-white blooms in Au-

gust. Thin to 5–10 stems for the largest flowers. Prefers moist soil. Height:
1.5–2m; width: 1.5–2. Sun to P.M. sun.

Larch 'Weeping'
Larix decidua 'Pendula'

Excellent feature tree for moist sites.
Graceful, weeping branches drape over
rocks and walls or crawl along the
ground. Soft green needles turn glow-
ing yellow and are shed in fall, growing
back each spring. Height: training dependant; width: 3–4m. Sun to P.M. sun.

Elder 'Black Beauty'

Arrowwood

Umbrella Plant

Larch 'Weeping'

Sweet Joe Pye

Marlene Willis keeps her pond clear of algae by growing a variety of water plants, such as horsetail, waterlily and cattail, which compete for light and nutrients.

My small pond always seems to have algae build–up even though I keep the circulating pump going constantly. I've heard that plants will help clear the water. What grows here?

CIRCULATING PUMPS ARE GREAT for keeping the water in a pond in motion and for adding oxygen to it, but they don't keep algae down. If you think about it, algae are really just miniature plants competing for the same resources as ornamental plants, namely nutrients, light and moisture. Reduce the resources available to algae and you'll reduce the algae. Pond plants are great competitors that use up the resources and occupy the space that algae try to monopolize. For the water in ponds to be clear, it must be balanced. Too many fish, which eat plants and produce waste, can cause nitrogen levels to increase, leading to prolific algae bloom. Fertilizer from lawns or flowerbeds leaching into the water can also create an imbalance—even using soil supplemented with fertilizer for potted pond plants can have an effect. Decaying vegetation releases nutrients that encourage algae growth, so promptly remove any dead or dying material from the water and keep pond plants trimmed of yellowing leaves. Partially shade the pond with floating plants, such as water lilies, and add oxygenating submersed plants (used at one bunch per 20 centimetres square) to colonize two-thirds of the pond.

SPRING BULBS

Canna Lily 'Pretoria' (Bengal Tiger)
Canna

This very unusual canna has huge melon-orange blooms. The striking foliage is striped yellow and green. Outstanding accent in the water garden or containers. Lift the bulb in fall to overwinter. Height: 90–120cm. Sun.

Canna Lily 'Stuttgart'
Canna

This tender bulb produces bright green foliage with wide white brush strokes on leaf edges. Produces small salmon flowers. Use in water gardens or containers. Lift the bulb in fall to overwinter. Height: 1.5m. Sun.

Elephant Ear 'Big Leaf'
Colocasia esculenta

An interesting bulb that makes an excellent large, tropical feature plant, producing huge, elephant ear-like foliage. Protect from hot sun and wind. Grows in water in its native habitat. Lift bulb to overwinter. Height: up to 2m. Shade to A.M. sun.

Elephant Ear 'Big Leaf'

Canna Lily 'Stuttgart'

Canna Lily 'Pretoria'

WATER PLANTS

Duckweed
Lemna spp.

A tiny floating plant with apple-green foliage that multiplies to cover the water's surface. It is easily kept in check by skimming off and discarding unwanted plants. It absorbs excess nutrients to help control algae, is hardy to Zone 3 and can over-winter in ice. Sun.

Frogbit
Hydrocharis morsus-ranae

This small floating plant has fleshy, water lily-like leaves and produces white flowers. It grows in clumps, and is a good oxygenator for small ponds. Sun.

Hornwort
Ceratophyllum

Dark green feathery foliage on long strands floats and grows along the bottom of the pond. Fish nibble on it and it is a good oxygenator. Usually sold in bundles.

Water Hyacinth and Duckweed

Parrots Feather

Hornwort

Narrowleaf Cattail
Typha angustifolia
This marginal plant has thin cattail leaves and does best when submerged no more than 30cm over the top of the pot. Hardy to Zone 2. Height: 2m. Sun to P.M. sun.

Parrots Feather
Myriophyllum aquaticum
Trailing stems with feathery green, needle-like leaves act as a very good green filter, using nutrients that would otherwise feed algae (also an oxygenator). Hardy to Zone 5 but may overwinter at a depth of 90cm below the ice. Cuttings can be brought indoors. Sun.

Water Hyacinth
Eichhornia crassipes
This floating plant has glossy, thick, fleshy leaves and will occasionally bloom producing lavender flowers—excellent at purifying the water. Overwinter indoors. Height: 5cm; width: 12cm. Sun.

Water Lettuce
Pistia stratiodes
This plant looks like a small cabbage floating on the pond surface. Its foliage is furry and ribbed. Height: 5cm; width: 12–15cm. Sun.

Water Lettuce

This bed, located adjacent to a sidewalk, is elegant in its simplicity and requires little maintenance.

Next to our garage is a narrow area, 1.5 metres wide by 6 metres long, that we pass through to access our back gate. It receives light most of the day and tends to be dry. I'd like to spruce it up, and to be honest, I'm not interested in putting too much effort into it. What grows here?

START OFF BY LAYING OUT a path to the gate. Choose from a wide range of simple paving stones that look great set out in an interesting (but simple) pattern. Next, select plants that don't require much care and attention. These can range from sturdy annuals and ground-covering creepers to a combination of small, drought-tolerant, narrowly shaped plants. Compact evergreens are particularly attractive and appealing to the low-maintenance gardener. Lastly, cover any bare ground, mulching around plants. This reduces weeding and watering considerably and gives a finished appearance to the area. If you are willing to put in a bit more effort at the beginning of the process, you'll end up with an attractive area that looks tidy and well groomed without much upkeep in the future.

ANNUALS

Amaranthus 'Pygmy Torch'

An exotic-looking plant that adds dramatic contrast to pots and flowerbeds. Produces 30cm spikes of deep crimson flowers. Warm location is a must for success. Superb cutflower. Height: 45–60cm; spacing: 30–40cm. Sun.

Rudbeckia 'Indian Summer'

A superb plant in mass displays, borders and containers. Produces loads of deep golden, semi-double, 15–25cm, daisy-like flowers with brown centres. Excellent cutflower. Height 50cm; spacing: 30cm. Sun.

PERENNIALS

Ground Ivy
Glechoma hederacea

Useful in covering large areas or growing between stepping stones—tolerates some foot traffic. Can be mowed over and doesn't require watering once established. Aggressive spreading habit with variegated foliage and blue to purple flowers in summer. Prefers fertile, well-drained soil. Height: 2–5cm; width: 45–90+cm. Sun or shade.

TREES & SHRUBS

Juniper 'Blue Arrow'
Juniperus scopulorum

This variety of juniper is extremely narrow and upright in habit, making it useful for framing entrances or as a feature plant. Displays intense deep blue foliage on a compact form that requires little or no shearing to maintain shape. Height: 5m; width: 60–90cm. Sun.

Pine 'White Bud'
Pinus mugo

An ideal small pine for small shrub beds and very heat tolerant. Naturally dense in habit and slow-growing—doesn't need pruning to maintain shape. Produces attractive white candles in spring. Height: 1m; width: 1m in 15–18 years. Sun to P.M. sun.

Potentilla 'Pink Beauty'
Potentilla fruticosa

Easy to grow with good heat and drought tolerance. Presents showy, long-lasting pink, semi-double blooms in summer on a compact, rounded form—great for borders or in mass plantings. Height: 60–75cm; width: 60–75cm. Sun to P.M. sun.

Pine 'White Bud'

Ground Ivy

Potentilla 'Pink Beauty'

9
Pests &
Diseases
Trouble in Paradise

I suppose in our technologically advanced world it's natural to assume that if your plants are infested with bugs or affected by diseases, the best way to deal with the problem is to apply a chemical. In truth all the pesticides and herbicides in the world won't help the situation if you don't understand the problem. Let's sum it up this way: know your enemy.

There is a common misconception that professional growers see an infestation of bugs, run to the chemical cabinet and blast the critters to smithereens. Reality is just the opposite. Professional growers spend far more time scouting for pest and disease problems, and doing everything in our power to prevent an outbreak before it starts, rather than applying expensive and time-consuming controls later. Take the time to regularly inspect plants in your garden—trust me, it's a lot easier to deal with three aphids than 3,000.

When we do spot a problem, we take time to identify the cause correctly before we develop a control strategy. Spraying is a last resort—and even then, we are careful to apply the appropriate product to the right plant, at the right time.

Choosing the best varieties is another great way to avoid pest and disease problems. Breeders have developed plants that are resistant to specific insect pests and diseases. Ask the staff at a reputable greenhouse to point these gems out. I once gave a gardening talk in Alaska and learned that a fungal disease called apple scab was a serious problem in the cool, moist climate of Alaska's coastal areas. According to the local experts, apple varieties that I knew performed well in my drier climate turned out to be very susceptible to scab there. I'm glad I learned that information before recommending varieties at my talk! This experience drove home the point that pest issues must always be taken into consideration on a regional basis.

The fact is there are no magic bullets when it comes to pest and disease control. The limited chemical pesticides currently available do come in handy in certain emergencies. But the cornerstone of pest control isn't chemical; it's knowledge.

IN THE GARDEN

I've had my own share of insect and disease problems. In the early years of market gardening, we noticed that many of our cabbage plants emerged well, but then grew steadily weaker.

We studied the plants and discovered incredibly thin and weak stems—soil nutrients and moisture couldn't reach the cabbage heads. Several textbooks later, the problem was diagnosed as wirestem, a disease caused by the fungus *Rhizoctonia solani*. We searched for solutions to find that heat killed off this seed-borne fungi, so we purchased nothing but heat-treated seed from that day forward.

Our wirestem problems became much less severe for just a few extra pennies per seed packet. Later on, we started growing wirestem-resistant varieties, which helped further quell the problem. Since then, we've always recommended spending the extra cash on top-quality seed and the best varieties.

A knot is formed as the fungus Dibotryon morbosum *causes the plant to produce tumour-like growths.*

I've always had trouble with black knot disease on many of my trees. I've removed quite a few over the years and don't want to grow any more that are susceptible. What grows here?

BLACK KNOT IS A SERIOUS DISEASE caused by the fungus *Dibotryon morbosum* (also known as *Apiosporina morbosa*). It affects trees in the *Prunus* genus, which includes cherries, plums and mayday. Knots become visible by the late summer of the year of infection, but are not usually noticed until the following spring, when they begin to enlarge rapidly. In the spring, the fungus produces spores that are carried on air currents and settle on the current season's growth of succulent green twigs, where they germinate and begin interrupting normal growth. A large black knot is formed as the fungus causes the plant to produce tumour-like growths. The fungus overwinters in these knots or in the infected wood immediately surrounding them. Black knot can be controlled using a combination of prevention and sanitation. Remove all knots and swellings by pruning 30 centimetres below the knot during the dormant season. Sterilize saws or pruners with a bleach solution between cuts and destroy the branches. A spray of lime sulfur applied as the tree is breaking dormancy may be helpful when pruning heavily infected trees.

FRUIT

Pear 'Golden Spice'
Pyrus

This lovely tree produces white blooms in spring followed by reddish-yellow, 5–6cm, sweet and aromatic pears in early October. The fruit is good for eating and processing. This variety is also fireblight resistant. Height: 5–6m; width: 4m. Sun.

TREES & SHRUBS

Amur Maackia
Maackia amurensis

Perfect for small yards and very showy. This globe-shaped tree's foliage is fine textured and it has golden bark. Creamy-white, fragrant flowers appear in midsummer. Plant in a sheltered site. Height: 6–10m; width: 6–7m. Sun.

Hawthorn 'Toba'
Crataegus x *mordenensis*

A beautiful, round-headed feature tree, great for small yards, screens or near decks—no thorns or fruit. Pink, fragrant, double blooms appear in spring. Height: 6m; width: 6m. Sun to P.M. sun.

Mountain Ash 'American'
Sorbus americana

This tree provides landscape interest all year. White flowers bloom in spring followed by clusters of bright orange-red fruit and stunning yellow-orange-red fall colour. A lovely round-headed, upright form that is great in small yards. Prefers well-drained soil. Height: 7–10m; width: 5–6m. Sun.

Ornamental Crabapple 'Royal Beauty'
Malus x 'Royal Beauty'

A spectacular ornamental, especially appropriate for a small yard. Deep greenish-purple-tinged foliage on a weeping form. Produces masses of pink blooms in late May and early June. Height: 4–5m; Width: 3m. Sun.

Willow 'Silver'
Salix alba var. *sericea*

A fast-growing feature tree for large yards or parks and acreages. Its newer branches are golden-coloured and the older bark is dark brown, contrasting nicely with the silver foliage. Prefers moist soil. Height: 9–10m; width: 7–10m. Sun.

Pear 'Golden Spice'

Hawthorn 'Toba'

Willow 'Silver'

Powdery mildew is unslightly and spreads quickly among drought-stressed and unhealthy plants.

The phlox I attempt to grow at the back of my yard along the fence always seems to be covered in powdery mildew. I've tried several varieties and now I'm ready to give up. What grows here?

P HLOX IS NOT THE ONLY PLANT that is affected by this problem—you'll see it on vegetables, shrubs, roses and numerous others. Powdery mildew is a fungus that grows on the surface of foliage, coating the plant with white felt-like mycelli that cause leaves to curl up and flower-buds to die without opening. The fungus spreads fastest among drought-stressed plants when evenings are cool and the air is humid and still. The spores rapidly germinate on leaves that have a film of moisture. New research indicates that enough of the spores can be washed off the leaves with lots of water to slow the spread of the fungus, but this strategy can lead to the development of other diseases. Space plants far enough apart to allow good air circulation and don't let them dry out between waterings. Keeping plants healthy and as vigorous as possible helps to prevent powdery mildew from invading foliage and flowers. The experts at your local garden centre should be able to recommend the most resistant cultivars of phlox and other powdery mildew-resistant plants.

ANNUALS

Petunia, Madness Series

Petunias are reliable plants for providing impact and colour from spring to early fall, whether in containers or planted out into the garden. The Madness series offers many shades of mixed, veined, 8cm, single flowers that are weather tolerant. Height: 25–30cm; spacing: 15–20cm. Sun to P.M. sun.

Salpiglossis, Royale Series

An exotic-looking bedding plant. This series produces a colour mix of extra large, trumpet-shaped flowers. Great used in large containers or as a striking garden plant. Makes an excellent cutflower. Height: 60cm; spacing: 20–30cm. Sun to P.M. sun.

PERENNIALS

False Sunflower
Heliopsis helianthoides

This large, clump-forming perennial is suitable for any mixed border and its blooms make excellent cutflowers. Single or double, golden-yellow flowers appear midsummer to fall. Prefers fertile, well-drained, moist, organic soil. Height: 1–1.5m; width: 60cm. Sun.

Salpiglossis, Royale Series

False Sunflower

Petunia, Madness Series

Garden Phlox

Phlox paniculata 'Becky Towe'

This variety is disease resistant and very showy, displaying an upright habit with gold-edged, variegated foliage. Large, showy and fragrant salmon-carmine flowers with a magenta eye appear in midsummer—makes a great cutflower. Deadhead to prolong flowering. Prefers moist, fertile, well-drained soil. Height: 50–75cm; width: 45–60cm. Sun to P.M. sun.

Garden Phlox

Phlox paniculata 'David'

This award-winning variety is mildew resistant and has an upright habit with strong sturdy stems. Huge fragrant, pure white flowers appear in midsummer. Prefers moist, fertile, well-drained soil. Height: 75–100cm; width: 45–60cm. Sun to P.M. sun.

Peony

Paeonia officinalis 'Alba Plena'

This group is generally more compact, blooms earlier and has thicker stems, which hold up better to adverse weather conditions. Double, white flowers, flushed pink appear in spring. Prefers moist, acid-free, fertile, well-drained soil. Clump-forming in habit. Height: 70–75cm; width: 60–90cm. Sun to P.M. sun.

Peony 'Alba Plena'

Garden Phlox 'Becky Towe'

Garden Phlox 'David'

Russian Sage
Perovskia atriplicifolia
This upright perennial has airy blue-mauve flowers in late summer atop aromatic, grey foliage and stems. Combine with other brightly coloured plants. Flowers are good for drying. A suitable plant for hot, dry sites. Prefers poor, to moderately fertile, well-drained soil, although it is tolerant of alkaline soils. Height: 75–100cm; width: 60–90cm. Sun.

Snowdrop Anemone
Anemone sylvestris
A colony-forming plant that is great for naturalizing in wild, woodland and contained areas. Produces fragrant nodding, pure white flowers in spring. Prefers moist, organic, fertile soil. Height: 30–50cm; width: 45–60+cm. Sun to P.M. sun.

ROSES

'Adelaide Hoodless' Parkland
Hardy Shrub
This lovely hardy rose is disease resistant producing flowers in clusters of up to 25. Hardy to Zone 2 with snow-cover. Double, red, 7cm flowers with a light fragrance bloom from June to frost. Height: 1.5–2m; width: 1.5–2m. Sun.

TREES & SHRUBS

Spiraea 'Magic Carpet'
Spiraea japonica
A great, low-growing contrast plant that produces red, yellow and pink blooms in June and July. Shearing plants after blooming encourages branching and fresh new colour. Height: 25–30cm; width: 60–90cm. Sun.

Russian Sage

'Adelaide Hoodless' Rose

Snowdrop Anemone

Spiraea 'Magic Carpet'

Fireblight, a highly infectious disease, causes leaves to curl up as if scorched and branches to display long black streaks.

Fireblight seems to be rampant in my area. I've seen it on many trees and I don't want to plant any more varieties that will be infected. What grows here?

BRANCHES INFECTED by this disease look like they've been scorched by flames; the wood displays long black streaks and leaves curl up. North America was, unfortunately, the launching point for fireblight problems worldwide (it was first identified in New York State in 1780) and now the disease has reached central Asia and New Zealand. It is the most highly infectious and devastating bacterial disease of apple, mountain ash and many other members of the rose family. The bacteria is called *Erwinia amylovora* (Latin for "starch eater") a descriptive title, because fireblight breaks down the starches in tree shoots, causing the scorched look. Some varieties of trees are more resistant to fireblight than others. Help prevent fireblight infection by avoiding excessive application of high nitrogen fertilizers that cause soft, leafy growth, which is more prone to fireblight attack, and avoid regular pruning of trees when the fireblight bacteria are abundant (i.e., spring and summer). Prune as soon as a branch becomes infected by cutting at least 20 centimetres below the visibly affected area, then destroying the infected branches. Disinfect pruning tools with bleach or ethanol between cuts to prevent further spread of this disease.

FRUIT

Pear 'Ure'
Pyrus

This small tree displays pretty white blooms each spring, followed by yellowish-green, 5cm, sweet and juicy, aromatic fruit, ripening mid to late September. The pears are good for cooking and eating. Height: 5–6m; width: 4m. Sun.

TREES & SHRUBS

Lilac 'Ivory Silk'
Syringa reticulata

A spectacular feature tree that blooms when most other trees have finished and its foliage contrasts wonderfully with blossoms of creamy-white to yellow in summer. Displays dark green leaves on an oval form that is suitable for small yards. Height: 10m; width: 10m. Sun.

Linden 'Morden Little-leaf'
Tilia cordata 'Morden'

A slower-growing tree, great in smaller yards. Has a straight, steel-grey coloured trunk and a nice narrow, upright, oval form. Fragrant yellow flowers appear in June/July. Height: 10m; width: 8m. Sun.

Maple 'Silver'
Acer saccharinum

Large leaves with silver-grey undersides are very showy in a breeze. This large, fast-growing, oval-shaped tree has a very dense canopy—excellent for shade. Great choice for wet sites. Height: 15–20m; width: 10–15m. Sun.

Ornamental Crabapple 'Big River'
Malus x 'Big River'

A perfect tree for the smaller yard with a pyramidal form. Great scale and fireblight resistance. Produces showy, 2–3cm, rose-pink, lightly fragrant blooms in May. Height: 6–7m; width: 2–3m. Sun.

Ornamental Crabapple 'Thunderchild'
Malus x *pumila*

Beautiful deep purple-red foliage and dark reddish-purple blooms in spring—excellent for small yards. Very resistant to fireblight. Height: 6–7m; width: 5–7m. Sun.

Linden 'Morden Little-leaf'

Maple 'Silver'

Left unchecked, the disease blackspot defoliates rosebushes and can sometimes even kill them.

All of my roses seem to get blackspot. I'm going to rip them all out and try new ones. There must be some roses that are resistant to this disease. What grows here?

BLACKSPOT IS ONE OF THE WORST diseases affecting roses. This fungus causes leaves to develop dark spots, then turn yellow and fall off. Left unchecked, blackspot defoliates rosebushes from the lower leaves up, and can sometimes even kill them. Blackspot is most infectious on warm, humid days, at temperatures of 20–24°C. The spores are spread by splashing water and germinate rapidly when they land on wet leaves. Always remember to water the soil, not the leaves! Good sanitation is a great preventive step; pick up and dispose of fallen leaves often, because they may harbour the fungus. The good news is that many rose varieties are resistant to blackspot. Interestingly, yellow roses, which are always the most popular among gardeners, seem to have a propensity for blackspot.

ROSES

'Captain Samuel Holland' Explorer
Shrub

A climbing rose with lots of flowers in clusters of up to 10. Hardy to Zone 3. Double, medium red, 7cm flowers bloom from early summer to frost. Light fragrance. Height: 2m; spread: 1–1.5m. Sun.

'David Thompson' Explorer
Hybrid Rugosa

The least thorny of the Explorer series. Classed as medium-red, but the colour is closer to deep fuschia. Double, medium red, 7–8cm flowers with a light fragrance bloom profusely July to frost. Height: 1m; width: 1m. Sun.

'Dwarf Pavement' Pavement
Hybrid Rugosa

A tough plant with a low, sprawling habit. Very salt-tolerant rose, named to reflect suitability for use as street-side plants. Offers mildly fragrant, semi-double, dark pink, 6–8cm flowers that repeat through summer. Height: 75–90cm; width: 90cm. Sun.

'Frau Dagmar Hartopp'
Hybrid Rugosa

A beautiful rose that is somewhat shade tolerant. Hardy to Zone 3, producing single, silver-pink, 8–10cm flowers with a strong rose fragrance repeatedly all summer. Height: 1m; width: 1.5m wide. Sun.

'Captain Samuel Holland' Rose

'Dwarf Pavement' Rose

'Frau Dagmar Hartopp' Rose

'David Thompson' Rose

'Frontenac' Explorer
Shrub

A short rose producing small clusters of blooms—hardy to Zone 3. Double, deep pink, 8cm flowers with a light fragrance bloom in June, repeating sporadically. Height: 75–90cm; width: 75–90cm. Sun.

'George Vancouver' Explorer
Shrub

Displays clustered blooms followed by 100's of red rosehips in fall—good resistance to mildew and blackspot. Har-

dy to Zone 3. Semi-double, medium red, 6cm flowers with a light fragrance bloom June through summer. Height: 60–75cm; width: 60–75cm. Sun.

'Henry Hudson' Explorer
Hybrid Rugosa

Blooms profusely—hardy to Zone 1. Double, appleblossom-white, 6–8cm flowers with a gentle fragrance bloom June through summer. Sun. Height: 60cm; width: 90–100cm. Sun.

'Frontenac' Rose

'Henry Hudson' Rose

'George Vancouver' Rose

'Jens Munk' Explorer
Hybrid Rugosa

Hardy to Zone 1. Double, medium pink marked with a striking white streak, 6–7cm flowers bloom abundantly all summer. Spicy fragrance. Height: 1.5m; width: 2m. Sun.

'Morden Blush' Parkland
Hardy Shrub

A very reliable, smaller rose—hardy to Zone 2. Blooms in clusters of up to 5 flowers. Double, ivory with blush pink centres, 7–8cm flowers with a soft fragrance bloom profusely from June to frost. Sun. Height: 60–90cm; width: 60–90cm. Sun.

'Quadra' Explorer
Hybrid Kordesii

An impressive climbing rose. Double, deep red buds open to rich red, 8–9cm flowers with a light, sweet fragrance from late June through summer. Height: 1.5–2m; width: 1m. Sun.

'Jens Munk' Rose

'Morden Blush' Rose

'Quadra' Rose

The whole organic movement is really about a balance between nature and man, embracing the philosophy of controlling, not eradicating, pests.

We have opted not to use any chemicals at all to control insect populations and disease problems on our plants. We would like to grow only plants that are disease and pest free. What grows here?

EVERYTHING IN THE WORLD is made up of chemicals, including our own bodies and every other living thing, so it would be a strange garden indeed that was chemical-free! Many gardeners choose to go "organic," but even so-called organic products contain ingredients that could be considered harmful to humans; organic and natural are not synonyms for good. Of course, what most people object to are not "chemical" pesticides, but rather commercially manufactured ones. A number of North American municipalities are banning popular garden products and there is a lot of debate surrounding this complicated issue. Gardeners who don't want to use chemical products might have to learn to change their expectations of gardening and their tolerance to bugs. The whole organic movement is really about a balance between nature and man, embracing the philosophy of controlling, not eradicating, pests. Fortunately, one of the goals of the horticulture industry is to produce plant varieties that are pest and disease resistant. Some plants just naturally seem to be tougher than others, but no plant is able to repel *every* insect and *every* disease. Keep your plants and soil healthy, catch pest problems early and you are well on your way to a better garden.

ANNUALS

Cosmos 'Sonata Mix'

This is a very trouble-free annual.
Rose-pink, candy-pink, white and
red, 10cm, daisy-like flowers bloom
all summer atop compact lacy foliage.
Wind tolerant. Height: 50–60cm; spacing: 25–30cm. Sun.

Lavatera 'Mont Blanc'

These bushy plants produce pure white,
large, single, hollyhock-like flowers—very showy in the garden. An
ideal feature plant that is wind tolerant
and rarely bothered by pests or disease.
Height: 60–90cm; spacing: 40–60cm.
Sun.

Lavatera 'Mont Blanc'

PERENNIALS

Golden Aster

Solidaster luteus

Rarely bothered by pests or disease
—a nice addition to a mixed border.
Produces clusters of yellow flowers
late summer to fall that make good
cutflowers. Prefers fertile, well-drained
soil—tolerates dry soil. Clump-forming
in habit. Height: 60–90cm; width:
20–30cm. Sun.

Golden Aster

Cosmos 'Sonata Mix'

Helen's Flower
Helenium autumnale

A reliable plant. Bright attractive flowers sit atop sturdy stems—superb in bouquets! Daisy-like, golden-yellow to copper-red flowers late summer to fall on clump-forming plants. Upright in habit. Prefers well-drained, fertile, moist soil. Height: 90cm–1.5m; width: 45–60cm. Sun to P.M. sun.

Hosta
Hosta 'Abiqua Drinking Gourd'

This hosta has large, cupped, thick, blue-green foliage—less attractive to slugs than other hostas. Clump-forming in habit. Prefers moist, fertile, well-drained, organic, slightly acidic soil. Height: 60cm; width: 1m. Shade to A.M. sun.

Hosta 'Abiqua Drinking Gourd'

Tomato 'Floramerica'

Spike Gayfeather
Liatris spicata

A lovely worry-free plant for the garden, *liatris* sports spiked, purple flowers in late summer that attracts bees and butterflies. An excellent cutflower. Upright in habit. Prefers moist, well-drained, moderately fertile soil. Height: 60–90cm; width: 30–45cm. Sun to P.M. sun.

TREES & SHRUBS

Cotoneaster 'Hedge'
Cotoneaster acutifolius

Also known as 'Peking.' A very hardy and useful shrub, traditionally sheared and shaped for formal hedging but equally as attractive left to arch in its natural form. Rarely bothered by pests. Plant 30–45cm apart for hedges. Dark green, dense foliage turns a lovely orange-red colour in fall. Height: 2–3m; width: 2–3m. Sun to P.M. sun.

Spike Gayfeather

Linden 'Boulevard'

Tilia americana 'Boulevard'

A fast-growing, hardy tree that is great for providing very dense shade. A great choice for large spaces. Produces masses of yellow, fragrant blooms in June/July. Height: 15–20m; width: 7–8m. Sun.

Wayfaring Tree

Viburnum lantana

This compact form is great for screening. Deep green leaves turn purple-red in fall and creamy-white blooms in May are very pretty. Height: 2–3m; width: 2–3 m. Sun.

VEGETABLES

Tomato 'Floramerica'

This is an award-winning tomato for outstanding disease resistance. Produces solid, deep red, large (200–300g) tomatoes. Flavour is wonderful fresh, canned or juiced. Matures in early August. Use a cage and do not prune. Sun.

Linden 'Boulevard'

Wayfaring Tree

Cotoneaster 'Hedge'

Understanding the life cycle of Delphinium worm (the larval stage of the leaf tier moth) is the key to controlling the damage it can inflict.

I've tried to grow delphiniums for years in my sunny garden, but every year they end up with green worms and I get few, if any, blooms. I'm tired of battling this pest. I want to grow tall perennials that will fill my beds and be pest free! What grows here?

I T'S EASY TO GET DISCOURAGED when you battle the same pest year after year. You could just stop growing a particular plant, but a little information about the pest may be all you need to control the situation. The green worm to which you refer is the larval stage of a moth called a leaf tier. The caterpillar ties up a mass of silk and leaves to protect itself and feeds on native larkspurs which belong to the delphinium family. Ornamental delphiniums are closely related to larkspur, so the leaf tier feeds on wild or garden varieties with equal zeal (it also enjoys monkshood). Fortunately, delphinium leaf tiers are as predictable as your next birthday. Just cut off the affected leaves in the spring, when the plants are around 30 centimetres tall, and stomp the bugs flat. By the time your plants re-grow, the bugs will have passed their feeding stage and won't pose a threat. Other tall perennials can fill the gaps left in your borders if you're determined to give up on delphiniums.

PERENNIALS

Common Betony
Stachys monieri 'Hummelo'
An upright plant that produces silver-grey, woolly foliage and pink to purple flowers in early summer to late summer. Prefers fertile, well-drained soil. Height: 25–50cm; width: 20–40cm. Sun to P.M. sun.

Culver's Root
Veronicastrum virginicum
Adds height to a mixed border and interesting texture with its whorls of leaves. Spiked, white to pink or bluish-purple flowers appear in summer. Prefers moist, fertile, organic soil. Clump-forming and upright in habit. Height: 60–180cm; width: 45cm. Sun to P.M. sun.

False Sunflower
Heliopsis helianthoides
This large, clump-forming perennial is suitable for any mixed border and its blooms make excellent cuflowers. Single or double, golden-yellow flowers appear in midsummer to fall. Prefers fertile, well-drained, moist, organic soil. Height: 1–1.5m; width: 60cm. Sun.

Globe Centaurea
Centaurea macrocephala
A very large, dominant plant for the back of the border. Produces large, fuzzy, thistle-like, yellow flowers in late-spring to late summer on shiny brown bracts. Attracts bees. Drought tolerant but prefers moist, fertile, well-drained soil. Clump-forming habit. Height: 90–150cm; width: 90–150cm. Sun to P.M. sun.

Globe Centaurea

False Sunflower

Culver's Root

Maltese Cross
Lychnis chalcedonica

A splash of brilliant red held atop up-right stiff stems—grow in a cottage garden or mixed border. Self-seeds and attracts hummingbirds. Cross-shaped, scarlet-red flowers bloom in early summer to midsummer. Prefers moist, fertile soil. Height: 90–120cm; width: 20–30cm. Sun to P.M. sun.

Obedient Plant
Physostegia virginiana

Plants stand up well to wind and produce lilac to purple-pink flow-ers in midsummer to fall—lovely as a cutflower. Has a spreading, upright habit with dark green, willowy foli-age. Prefers moist, fertile soil. Height: 60–100cm; width: 45–60cm. Sun.

Plume Poppy
Macleaya cordata

This big, upright plant is useful as a background or feature plant in a mixed border. Large, heart-shaped, blue-grey leaves are very tropical looking. Produces cream plumes in summer. Tolerates some shade and prefers deep, fertile, moist, well-drained soil. Height: 1.5–2m; width: 90–100cm. Sun to P.M. sun.

Plume Poppy

Obedient Plant

Maltese Cross

Small Globe Thistle
Echinops ritro

A heat-tolerant addition to a border or wild garden. Silver-grey foliage is clump-forming and compact in habit. Blue flowers appearing in late summer attract butterflies and are excellent for cutting and drying. Thrives in poor, well-drained soil. Height: 60cm; width: 45 cm. Sun to P.M. sun.

Spike Gayfeather
Liatris spicata 'Goblin'

A lovely dwarf variety of liatris sporting spiked, purple flowers in late summer that attract bees and butterflies. An excellent cutflower. Upright in habit. Prefers moist, well-drained, moderately fertile soil. Height: 45–60cm; width: 30–45cm. Sun to P.M. sun.

Sweet Joe Pye
Eupatorium purpureum

One of the showiest perennials. It forms a large, clump-forming, upright bush that contrasts well with evergreens and attracts butterflies. Fragrant, clustered, rose-purple flowers bloom late in summer to fall. Prefers moist, alkaline soil. Height: 90–150cm; width: 90–100cm. Sun to P.M. sun.

Small Globe Thistle

Spike Gayfeather 'Goblin'

Sweet Joe Pye

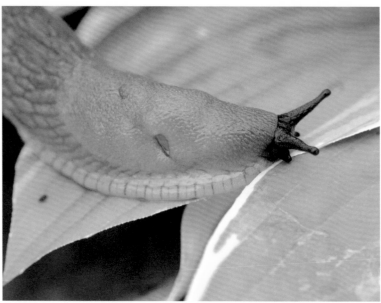

Growing plants that are unpalatable to slugs is a practical approach to eliminating them from the garden.

We landscaped last year and now have a beautiful garden. Unfortunately, slugs seem to be enjoying it as well and are eating quite a few of our new hostas and other plants all over the yard. We'd like to grow plants that won't be consumed by these pests. What grows here?

YOU MAY HAVE INCORPORATED features that readily welcome and harbour slugs without even realizing it. Decks, mulched beds and even stepping stones provide places for slugs to hide during the heat of the day, only to emerge to eat holes in leaves, stems and flowers, leaving a silvery trail behind. Gardeners use all kinds of methods to deter these slimy visitors. Some of the most popular methods are applying iron phosphate, laying down copper "fences," which slugs won't cross, using slug traps baited with beer and trapping them under boards to collect and destroy each morning. Another approach is to surround plants that are slug favourites with plants that slugs dislike. The most practical approach, though, is to grow plants that are unpalatable to slugs. Slugs and snails tend to avoid plants with hairy leaves and those that contain certain chemical compounds. It would be a shame to give up on an entire group of plants, so don't give up on hostas, but choose the thick-leaved varieties.

ANNUALS

Ageratum, Hawaii Series

This annual makes an attractive edging around beds and is excellent in compact borders. Displays striking clusters of feathery flowers. Available in individual colours or as a mix. Height: 15cm; spacing: 10–15cm. Sun to P.M. sun.

Rudbeckia 'Prairie Sun'

This plant offers a lot of colour impact in the garden or containers. Golden-yellow, 12cm, green-eyed, daisy-like flowers are held atop sturdy stems on a plant with a stocky habit—excellent cutflowers. Often used in mass displays. Height: 90cm; spacing: 40–45cm. Sun.

Ageratum 'Hawaii Blue'

FALL BULBS

Allium 'Globemaster'

Beautiful, large (25cm) umbels of lavender blooms are held atop tall, stiff stems—very attractive planted among shrubs and perennials. Flowers do not produce seed, so they last longer. Prefers well-drained, sandy soil. Height: 100cm: space 6–8cm apart. Sun.

Allium 'Globemaster'

Rudbeckia 'Prairie Sun'

Galanthus (Snowdrop)
Galanthus nivalis

Honey scented, single, pendulous, bell-shaped, white flowers with green accents on inner petals appear in very early spring. This species naturalizes easily. The most cold-tolerant snowdrop, and disliked by rodents and squirrels. It requires cool, moist conditions for the summer dormant period. Prefers moist, fertile soil. Height: 8–10 cm; plant 8–10cm deep and 6–8cm apart. P.M. sun.

Goldvein Iris

Galanthus

Bethlehem Sage
Pulmonaria saccharata

Pulmonarias are very tough, clump-forming plants that are well suited as groundcovers for a woodland or border edging. Blue flowers appear in spring, but these plants are prized for their spotted foliage. Prefers fertile, well-drained, organic soil but will tolerate poor soil. Height: 20–30cm; width: 45–60cm. Shade to A.M. sun.

Fumitory
Corydalis lutea

A mounding perennial with evergreen, fern-like foliage—do not cut back. Produces tubular yellow flowers late-spring to summer. May reseed. Prefers fertile, well-drained soil. Height: 20–40cm; width: 30cm. Shade to A.M. sun.

Bethlehem Sage

Goldvein Iris
Iris chrysographes

A beautiful garden iris with elegant markings. Greyish-green foliage displays fragrant, reddish-violet flowers with gold streaks on falls in early summer. Prefers moist, organic soil. Clump-forming in habit. Height: 40–50cm; width: 30–45cm. Sun to P.M. sun.

Great Masterwort
Astrantia major

This clump-forming plant is very nice used in a woodland or mixed border. Whitish-green to rose-red flowers appear in summer and make excellent dried flowers. Prefers moist, fertile, organic soil but will tolerate drier sites. Height: 40–60cm; width: 60–90cm. Sun to P.M. sun.

Showy Stonecrop
Sedum spectabile

This thick-stemmed, clump-forming and upright sedum produces clustered pink flowers in late summer to fall. Very attractive in fall. Prefers well-drained, moderately fertile soil but is quite tolerant of poor soils and dry periods. Height: 30–45cm; width: 45–60cm. Sun to P.M. sun.

Wild Blue Phlox
Phlox divaricata 'Plum Perfect'

A wonderful groundcover for shady gardens that tolerates some sun and dryness once established. This variety is mildew and slug resistant. Semi-evergreen foliage forms a loose mat with a spreading habit. Fragrant plum-purple flowers with a darker eye bloom in spring to early summer. Cut back after flowering. Prefers moist, fertile, organic, neutral to acidic soil. Height: 20–40cm; width: 30–45+cm. Shade to A.M. sun.

Wild Blue Phlox 'Plum Perfect'

Showy Stonecrop

Great Masterwort

These strange-looking growths on a maple leaf are caused by eriophyid mites.

My maple trees have developed long finger-like projections on their leaves. I'm told they are galls caused by mites. I don't want to grow any other plants that will be affected by this unsightly problem. What grows here?

MICROSCOPIC ORGANISMS called eriophyid mites cause the strange-looking growths you've seen on your maples, but there are many other types that attack other plants. When eriophyid mites feed on the leaves, they secrete a substance that causes leaves to swell and encapsulate the mites. Once the lumps and bumps appear, there's almost no way to control them. Fortunately, apart from the cosmetic damage, the mites don't cause any significant harm in a single season, but repeated severe infestations can weaken a tree and contribute to its death. If you've had infestations in the past, begin treatment at the tight bud stage, in the spring by spraying the tree with dormant oil or a miticide.

TREES & SHRUBS

Birch 'Cutleaf Weeping'
Betula pendula 'Lacinata'
A very graceful, weeping form with deeply cut leaves that create a fine textured look on long, arching branches reaching the ground. The bark is a beautiful bright white. Produces catkins in the spring. Thrives in moist soil. Height: 15m; width: 6–10m. Sun.

Black Walnut
Juglans nigra
A beautiful, long-lived feature tree displaying coarse, fern-like foliage on a very large, round-headed form. Use in large yards. Does best in deep, rich soil. Height: 15–25m; width: 10–15m. Sun.

Lilac 'Japanese Tree Lilac'
Syringa reticulata
A spectacular feature tree that blooms when most other trees have finished and its foliage contrasts wonderfully with blossoms of creamy-white to yellow in summer. Displays dark green leaves on an oval form that is suitable for small yards. Usually sold in a multi-stemmed form. Height: 10m; width: 10m. Sun.

Mountain Ash 'American'
Sorbus americana
This tree provides landscape interest all year. White flowers bloom in spring followed by clusters of bright orange-red fruit and stunning yellow-orange-red fall colour. A lovely round-headed, upright form that is great in small yards. Prefers well-drained soil. Height: 7–10m; width: 5–6m. Sun.

Ohio Buckeye
Aesculus glabra
This large, round-headed tree provides heavy shade and is best suited to large yards. Clustered creamy blooms in late spring are followed by interesting nuts covered with large spines. Produces super fall colour. Height: 10–15m; width: 10–15m. Sun to P.M. sun.

Russian Olive
Elaegnus angustifolia
A round-headed, small tree that is also sold in shrub form. Silvery leaves and dark bark contrast well with evergreen backgrounds. Very fragrant, tiny, yellow blooms appear in June. Thrives in a hot, dry site. Height: 6–10m; width: 6–10m. Sun.

Mountain Ash 'American'

10
Small Spaces

Another Dimension

Space is precious, whether at a large commercial operation or on an apartment balcony. While home gardeners don't have to worry about making money from their plants, they do want to take full advantage of the space they have and give their plants what they need.

At our greenhouse, we've spent years learning how best to use our growing space and therefore get the most value from it. We've figured out the minimum space needed to grow high-quality plants—and found some pretty creative places to grow them. For us, the trick is to grow them as close together as possible, thereby maximizing the number we can offer for sale, while leaving enough space between the plants to avoid undue competition for light.

We grow flats of plants on the heated floor of our growing range, pots of trailing plants in troughs mounted between support posts and on walls, and hanging baskets suspended from the roof. We use every bit of space and available light to our advantage. You can do it too by maximizing the efficiency of your yard and experimenting with spacing. Fill your beds with varieties of plants that really perform—don't waste time and energy on those that don't deliver. Use vertical surfaces; grow plants up walls and fences, try growing zucchini up an obelisk, instead of allowing it to sprawl across the ground (you'll gain space to grow other plants). Use patios or decks to grow containers of herbs, vegetables or bedding plants, and take advantage of hanging baskets—they're incredibly efficient space-savers that look terrific when hung from tree branches, fences, the eaves of your home or even the post that holds up your clothesline.

The point is to use the space you have as efficiently and effectively as possible, whether you're growing ten thousand geraniums in a retail greenhouse or herbs in a window box. You'll always come out ahead if you manage your space carefully—and more importantly, *creatively*.

IN THE GARDEN

Bob Stadnyk enthusiastically gardens in the very tiny yard of his condominium. Every time he comes across a new plant he desires (which is fairly often), he's faced with the problem of finding a spot—any spot—in which to grow it. Bob's response to his space restrictions is twofold: he uses every spare centimetre available to him, and he is selective about what he grows.

In the only open area of the yard, Bob created an alpine bed and filled it with an incredibly diverse collection of small beautiful plants. Now that this garden is full to the brim, he must limit new plant selections to the very smallest, slowest-growing varieties of the plants he really wants.

Bob makes extensive use of his deck as a growing space by planting up pots with a wide array of perennials, bedding plants, vegetables and a prized Japanese maple. He even uses the fence and the underside of an open staircase for hanging baskets.

Bob's small but gorgeous garden is always evolving and, far from inhibiting his creativity, the limited space has helped Bob create a cozy, surprisingly diverse yard.

If you have a tiny yard and want to grow fruiting plants consider 'Evans' cherry—a smallish tree that produces big, tasty fruit.

I have a really small yard, but I have always wanted to have both an orchard *and* a flowering border. I'd like to combine the two, but I don't want to use a ladder to harvest fruit because it will damage the surrounding flowering plants. What grows here?

I T IS POSSIBLE FOR YOU TO GROW a variety of fruiting trees in your small yard, and your concerns about harvesting without damaging surrounding plants can be dealt with by eliminating the need for a ladder altogether. Simply grow smaller fruiting plants. There are several varieties of apples available that are grafted to create a dwarf-form tree that produces full-size fruit; there are also other reasonably small fruit trees that can be kept pruned to a tidy form. Space these trees far enough apart to allow the border you desire and plot a path around each one, making an opening wide enough to walk through for harvesting and pruning. When you select ornamental plants, consider the size of these diminutive trees and choose varieties that won't grow any larger than half the tree's height to maintain visual balance in the yard. Remember that fruit trees bloom in spring, so consider adding some spring-blooming bulbs to your border to create a spectacular display.

FRUIT

Apple 'Dwarf Battleford'
Malus

Dwarf apple trees are perfect for the small yard or yards with limited space. Tests done in Saskatchewan have shown this rootstock to be extremely hardy. These trees will grow 20–25% of their normal size, but will bear fruit more consistently than on regular rootstock. Battleford apples are crisp and tasty, maturing in early September. The 7–8cm, red with green stripes fruit is a fair keeper that is good for desserts and fair for cooking. Height: 3m; width: 1.5–2m. Sun.

Blueberry 'Chippewa'
Vaccinum

This variety produces high yields (4–7kg) of tasty large berries in late July/early August that are great to eat fresh or to cook with. One of the hardiest of all blueberries. Offers great fall colour. Prefers moist, acidic soil and benefits from winter snowcover. Self-pollinating. Height: 1m; width: 1m. Sun.

Cherry 'Evans'
Prunus cerasus

This self-pollinating, sour cherry displays pretty white blooms in spring, followed by bright red, 2–3cm, sweet-tart fruit in late July/early August. Delay harvest to increase sugars—excellent for fresh eating, pies and wine-making. Height: 3–4m; width: 2–3m. Sun.

Cherry 'Nanking'
Prunus

This is a versatile cherry often used as an ornamental for hedges or trained to small tree form. Pretty pink blooms in early spring are followed by 4–11kg yields of 2cm, sweet cherries. Use for pies, jellies or enjoy eating fresh. Height: 2–3m; width; 2–3m. Sun.

Cherry Plum 'Convoy'
Prunus

This useful little cherry pollinates other mid season cherries and plums. It produces white blooms followed by 2cm, scarlet fruit with yellow flesh in mid August. Good for canning and jams. Height: 2–3m; width: 2–3m. Sun.

Jostaberry
Ribes

This vigorous-growing, black currant and gooseberry cross is very productive, showing good mildew resistance. Black, 2cm fruit matures in June to July—great for fresh eating and processing. Height: 90cm; width: 90cm. Sun.

Blueberry 'Chippewa'

Cherry 'Nanking'

Jostaberry

Make the most of available gardening space in a tiny yard by growing ornamental and edible plants together in beds and containers as Bob Stadnyk, our perennial manager, does.

I have a tiny yard to the rear of a condominium. It is only 5 metres by 5 metres, with a portion of the space being taken up by my wooden deck. I would like to grow blooming plants and have a vegetable garden, but I can't seem to figure out how to have both. What grows here?

Y OU NEED TO THINK about gardening in less traditional terms. Ornamental plants and vegetables can be combined to maximize limited space—they don't have to exist separately. Also, consider the fact that many plants grown for ornamental value are actually edible (such as pansies and nasturtiums) and that many edibles have ornamental value (such as shrub cherries and blueberries). Utilize every inch of space in your yard, including the deck (for pots filled with fragrant herbs), the walls of the condominium (for hanging baskets) and the fence (for climbing plants). You really can have it all—maybe just not as much of it!

ANNUALS

Bachelor's Button, Finest Series

This attractive annual self-seeds readily—an excellent cutflower and edible (add to salads). Pretty blue, pink or white blooms. Height: 90cm; spacing: 15–20cm. Sun.

Chard 'Bright Lights'

This variety is ornamental with very attractive, bright-coloured veins and stalks. It is edible, offering delicious foliage. Makes a striking accent plant in containers or the artful vegetable garden. Height: 30cm; spacing: 20–25cm. Sun.

Nasturtium, Whirlybird Series

All parts of nasturtium are edible and can be added to salads and cakes. This series offers semi-double, upward facing blooms held well above the foliage. Available in shades of cherry-rose, gold, mix, orange and scarlet. Height: 15–20cm; spacing: 15–20cm. Sun to P.M. sun.

Pansy, Whiskers Series

Pansies thrive in early spring and late fall due to their exceptional frost tolerance. Great in pots or planted out in the garden—excellent garden performance. This series offers 6–7cm flowers in bright colours with contrasting whiskers. Height: 15–20cm; spacing: 20–25cm. Sun to P.M. sun.

Bachelor's Button 'Finest Blue'

Pansy 'Whiskers Purple-White'

Nasturtium, Whirlybird Series

FRUIT

Blueberry 'Northland'
Vaccinum

This variety produces high yields (4–7kg) of tasty berries in late July/early August that are great to eat fresh or to cook with. Blueberry shrubs also provide striking foliage colour in the fall. Prefers moist, acidic soil and benefits from winter snowcover. Height: 1m; spread; 1.5–2m. Sun.

Cherry 'Carmine Jewel'
Prunus x *kerrasis*

An extremely hardy, Saskatchewan introduction that is beautiful and practical. Ornamental white blooms appear in spring followed by dark red skinned and fleshed, 3–4cm cherries in mid July/mid August—great for processing. Height: 2–3m; width: 2–3m. Sun.

PERENNIALS

Common Hops
Humulus lupulus

This vigorous vine requires a strong support for its climbing habit and will cover a large area. Produces coarse, large foliage and cone-like, green, female flowers in summer. Cut back in fall. Prefers well-drained, organic, moderately fertile, moist soil. Height: 4–6m; width 2–3+m. Sun to P.M. sun.

Cherry 'Carmine Jewel'

Blueberry 'Northland'

Common Hops

VEGETABLES

Bean Scarlet Runner

A very ornamental and vigorous pole bean. The vines sport scarlet flowers followed by green, 15cm beans. Can be grown up poles, trellises and fences. Late July to early August harvest. Height: 2–3+m. Sun.

Lettuce Red 'Rage'

Crinkly, deep red leaves on a compact form characterize this sweet and tasty lettuce. Adds great contrast to a garden. Matures in early July but keep sowing for a continuing harvest. Sun to A.M. shade.

Tomato 'Tumbler'

Produces the heaviest yields of any tomato relative to the plant's size— excellent in large hanging baskets and pots. Offers an abundance of small, tasty, cherry tomatoes maturing in early July. A heavy feeder, requiring fertilizing at every watering with 15-15-30. Sun.

Tomato 'Tumbler'

Bean Scarlet Runner

Lettuce Red 'Rage'

No mattter the size of your garden, choosing the highest yielding varieties of vegetables will make the most efficient use of the space.

I have a 3 metre by 3 metre vegetable plot. My father-in-law says he has heard that by planting the right vegetables in tight blocks, I can get the same harvest as a much larger garden. What grows here?

THIS CONCEPT IS KNOWN as intensive planting and/or square-foot gardening. The idea is that by sectioning off blocks of the garden and seeding or planting closely, yields can be as high as those from gardens that are larger, where seeding and planting is wider spaced. Proponents of this concept feel that it is less time-consuming, because weeds have little space to invade. Starting off with good quality-soil is really important to meet the high nutrient requirements that intensive planting demands. The principle of square-foot gardening is that bare ground is wasted ground, but don't forget that you still need at least a little space between plants to hoe, harvest and to allow room for growth. This may take a little experimentation on your part, based on the different varieties you grow. Your father-in-law is correct that choosing the best, highest-yielding varieties of plants can make a big difference in what you reap—no matter the size of the vegetable garden you plant.

VEGETABLES

Bean 'Strike'

An outstanding bush bean, yielding quantities of tasty, deep green, long, (10–15cm) slim, tender beans that mature mid to late July. Plants are compact and no staking is required. Sun.

Carrot 'Baby Sweet'

The ultimate baby carrot. Very sweet and juicy, coreless, short carrots that do not require peeling. Matures very early form mid to late July. Sow for continuous harvest. Sun.

Cucumber 'Fanfare'

An award-winning slicing variety that produces over a long period of time, with fruit maturing beginning as early as late July. Produces slim, dark green, flavourful cucumbers up to 20–25cm long. Small plants with excellent yields—great for container growing. Needs only 60cm of garden space. Sun.

Onion 'Long White Summer Bunching'

This onion produces upright, white shafts, 13–18cm in length. It does not bulb—great addition to salads. Sun.

Pepper 'The Big Early'

An absolutely huge and flavourful green pepper. Fruit grows up to 20cm long by 11cm wide—great for stuffing. Very good yields per plant. Cage plants to support and maximize garden space. Sun.

Tomato 'Golden Girl'

This bush-type tomato has very high yields of 200–300g, smooth, golden yellow tomatoes. Flavour is sweet and mild. Use a cage and do not prune. Sun.

Zucchini 'Space Miser'

An extremely early and prolific variety, producing deep green and uniformly sized zucchinis. Plants are compact and excellent for smaller vegetable gardens. Sun.

Zucchini 'Space Miser'

Tomato 'Golden Girl'

Pepper 'The Big Early'

With regular fertilizing, watering and quality soilless mix, container-grown plants will thrive on a balcony.

I have tried to grow a few vegetables and herbs in containers on my sunny, hot balcony. They didn't do very well, even though I used good topsoil in my pots. Perhaps I tried the wrong ones. What grows here?

THE BIGGEST MISTAKE BALCONY gardeners make is to use containers that are too small and to fill them with garden soil or topsoil. Always use good-quality potting soil and choose the largest containers you can fit in your space. Field soil is great in the field, but it's not so great in pots. It's heavy, gets compacted easily, and often contains weed seeds, diseases and insect pests. Soilless mixtures are a far better choice for pots. Use supports such as tomato cages to combat wind, and think vertically when planting to utilize the space fully. Keep in mind that container-grown vegetables require extra watering and fertilizing to produce the best yields. You may have to water as often as twice a day in the heat of summer, and remember to apply fertilizer once a week. We like to add a pinch to the watering can each time we water. Be a good neighbour and use saucers under your containers to hold water and stop dripping to the apartment below.

VEGETABLES

Broccoli 'Munchkin'

A space saving variety—grows well in large containers. Produces deep blue-green, finely beaded heads. After harvesting the main heads, good-sized secondary heads develop. Matures in about 60 days. Height: 30cm: spacing: 15–30cm. Sun.

Eggplant 'Little Fingers'

This variety is spineless which makes it much easier to pick the 10–15cm long eggplants. Produces high yields of dark purple fruit—maturing in late July. Sun.

Lettuce 'Bon Vivant'

A beautiful mix of salad greens in a full range of colours and textures. Includes deep red, bronze and light green to deep green lettuce. Can be eaten when only a few centimeters tall up to full size. Matures late June to early July. Seed every 14 days for a continuous harvest. Sun to A.M. sun.

Pepper 'Early Sunsation'

This early bell pepper performs really well in a container and in short season locations. Plants are loaded with medium-sized peppers that mature very early. Fruit starts out green, maturing to gold. Sun.

Sweet Potato 'Georgia Jet'

This variety produces high yields of tubers that can be harvested early. The sweet potatoes are rosy skinned and the flesh is orange and moist. Let dry for 2–3 weeks before storing and using. Sun.

Tomato 'Tiny Tim'

Compact—plant a few in a big container. Produces bright red, tasty fruit with terrific flavour. Matures early July. No pruning or support required, but in windy situations a cage is helpful. Sun.

Lettuce 'Bon Vivant'

Eggplant 'Little Fingers'

Broccoli 'Munchkin'

The number of evergreens available today from well-stocked and specialty nurseries is so vast that you're sure to find varieties to fit the size of your yard.

I want to create a replica of a beautiful evergreen bed that I saw while on holiday in the Pacific northwest. The problem is that my yard is only about a quarter of the size of the bed that I admired, and I'm sure my zone is colder. What grows here?

DOESN'T IT SEEM THAT GARDENERS will grab inspiration from wherever they travel in the world? If you took pictures on your holiday, study them to see what it is that you like most about the bed. It could be the way the plant shapes relate to each other, the way the colours of the foliage work together or the interesting combination of textures. Maybe it's all these things that please your eye. Although you may not be able to duplicate the bed with the same plants, you can capture its feel by using evergreens that are smaller but have the same forms and colours. Well-stocked garden centres and specialty nurseries carry a variety of evergreens in many sizes; prairie gardeners have about 300 to choose from, and many are new, tough varieties, including spruces, pines, junipers, cedars, boxwood. You'll probably exhaust your budget long before you even skim the surface of available varieties! Shop early in the season, as many retail outlets sell out of these plants quickly.

PERENNIALS

Bunchberry
Cornus canadensis

This evergreen groundcover is good for naturalizing a shady area. Cream flowers in summer are followed by bright red, edible berries in fall. Prefers moist, acidic soil. Height: 10–20cm; width: 30+cm. Shade to A.M. sun.

TREES & SHRUBS

Cedar 'Danica'
Thuja occidentalis

A tiny, slow-growing cedar, displaying bright green foliage, tinged blue in winter. A round, compact form—very nice addition to a rock garden or evergreen bed. Height: 45cm; width: 45–60cm in 20 years. Sun to P.M. sun.

Falsecypress 'Thread-Leaf'
Chamaecyparis pisifera 'Filifera'

An excellent feature plant with attractive, long, thread-like foliage on a mounding form, maturing to a broad pyramid shape. Best planted in a wind-sheltered site. Requires moist soil. Height: 12–15m; width: 3–6m. Sun to P.M. sun.

Falsecypress 'Thread-Leaf'

Cedar 'Danica'

Bunchberry

Juniper 'Blue Forest'

Juniperus sabina

This lovely juniper sports dark blue foliage with branches whose ends curl straight up like a dwarf forest—makes a striking groundcover. Height: 15–30cm; width: 1.5–2m. Sun.

Juniper 'Blue Star'

Juniperus squamata

Very bright blue foliage on a slow-growing, rounded bush that does not require pruning to maintain its attractive form. Best with good snowcover through winter. Height: 90cm; width: 1–1.5m. Sun.

Juniper 'Lime Glow'

Juniperus horizontalis

This variety holds its colour well with feathery new foliage opening lime green on a vase-shaped form. Tolerant of dry sites once established. Offers great colour contrast in a mixed bed. Height: 60–90cm; width: 1.5–2m. Sun to P.M. sun.

Pine 'Columnar Scotch'

Pinus sylvestris 'Fastigiata'

Very dense foliage with a rich, steely blue colour on a very narrow form—great as a feature or framing entrances and driveways. Height: 7–9m; width: 45–60cm. Sun.

Pine 'Columnar Scotch'

Juniper 'Blue Star'

Spruce 'Acrocona'
Picea abies

An absolutely spectacular spruce—showy! Exceptional reddish-purple cones are borne on the branch ends of this broad and pyramidal form. A great feature tree for an evergreen bed. Height: 2–3m; width: 2–3m in 10–12 years. Sun.

Spruce 'Iseli Columnar Blue'
Picea pungens 'Iseli Fastigiate'

This spruce has a very narrow, upright form—great for flanking a driveway or house entrance or as an accent in a shrub bed. Compact, steel-blue foliage is beautiful. Excellent selection for small yards. Height: 10–20m; width: 3–4m. Sun.

Yew 'Dwarf Japanese'
Taxus cuspidata 'Nana'

A low-growing, compact yew that offers excellent colour contrast in shrub borders and foundation plantings. Very tolerant of shearing. Requires moist soil. Height: 60–90cm; width: 60–90cm. Shade to A.M. sun.

Spruce 'Acrocona'

Spruce 'Iseli Columnar Blue'

Yew 'Dwarf Japanese'

Index

About the Author

Inheriting his mother's love of horticulture, **Jim Hole** grew up gardening. After earning a Bachelor of Science in Agriculture with a major in Plant Science, Jim and his brother Bill helped develop Hole's Greenhouses & Gardens, which was founded by their parents Ted and Lois, into one of the largest retail greenhouse operations in Canada. Jim appears regularly on CBC radio and television call-in shows to share what he's learned from over 30 years of hands-on experience in the greenhouse.

Jim's interest has always centred on the science within the garden—explaining what makes plants tick with a clear and concise style, without losing sight of the beauty and wonder that makes gardening worthwhile.

Jim regularly contributes articles to several national magazines and writes a weekly gardening column for the *Edmonton Journal*. He is a frequent speaker at gardening groups and trade shows across North America. Jim is the author of *What Grows Here? Volume 1: Locations* and is the co-author, with his mother Lois, of five *Question and Answer* books and was the driving force behind the creation of *Lois Hole's Favorite Bulbs*.

For more from Jim Hole, including his speaking schedule, columns and gardening tips, visit www.enjoygardening.com.

The success of this book is due entirely to the hard work of the staff of Hole's Greenhouses and Gardens over the years, including, but not limited to…

Christina McDonald
EDITOR

Gregory Brown
DESIGN

Akemi Matsubuchi
PRINCIPAL PHOTOGRAPHY

Christina McDonald & Earl J. Woods
CONTRIBUTING WRITERS

Jan Goodall, Valerie Hole, Dorothy Jedrasik,
Maggie Neilson, Shane Neufeld & Bob Stadnyk,
HORTICULTURAL RESEARCH & CONSULTATION

Bruce T. Keith & Leslie Vermeer
EDITORIAL CONSULTANTS

Acknowledgements

We are grateful to all the gardeners who so generously opened their yards to us to photograph, and who shared their ideas and solutions to many gardening challenges.

Beth and Grant Anderson
Peg Barcelo-Jackson
Bernd Becker
Donna and George Bellemar
Mike and Colleen Brezovski
Russel Burke
Calgary Zoo
John Chan and Lorne Warneke
Maggie Clayton
CNIB Calgary Branch
Dr. Michael Coe
Carolyn and Tim Dryden
Judith Fraser
Tom and Susan Folkert
Guy Fortier
Connie Fry
Ed and Viky Gartner
Dave Grice
Irene Groves
Rene Haasdyk
Vivien and Ken Hayes
Don Heimbrecher
Jeanne and Jim Irwin
Susan and Mike Jacka

Colleen Jackson
Bruce Keith and Leslie Vermeer
Pat Lewis and Matt O'Reilly
Felicia Carrera-Lowe, Ian Visman
  and daughter Lilia
Elissa Marchant
Peter Maskell
Hisaye Matsubuchi
Christi and Dan Mattiussi
John and Kay Melville
Tim Morrison and Roxanne Bunyan
Maggie Nielson
Chris and Jim Newton
Penny and Dave Odegard
Felicity Pickard
Stephen Raven
Dana Rodgers
Karen Rotniak
Bob Stadnyk
Leona Stewart
Bryan Todd
Tal and Gigi Talibi
Marlene Willis
Chris and Cathy Zaychuk
Debra and Herb Zechel